BestMasters

Springer awards „BestMasters" to the best master's theses which have been completed at renowned Universities in Germany, Austria, and Switzerland.
The studies received highest marks and were recommended for publication by supervisors. They address current issues from various fields of research in natural sciences, psychology, technology, and economics.
The series addresses practitioners as well as scientists and, in particular, offers guidance for early stage researchers.

More information about this series at http://www.springer.com/series/13198

Fabian Regele

Infrastructure Investments

Regulatory Treatment and Optimal Capital Allocation Under Solvency II

Springer Gabler

Fabian Regele
Frankfurt am Main, Germany

BestMasters
ISBN 978-3-658-20163-0 ISBN 978-3-658-20164-7 (eBook)
https://doi.org/10.1007/978-3-658-20164-7

Library of Congress Control Number: 2017959882

Springer Gabler

Printed on acid-free paper

This Springer Gabler imprint is published by Springer Nature
The registered company is Springer Fachmedien Wiesbaden GmbH
The registered company address is: Abraham-Lincoln-Str. 46, 65189 Wiesbaden, Germany

Preface

Infrastructure investments are frequently characterized as long-term investments generating stable cash flows, offering a good diversification potential as well as a sound protection against inflation. These attributes indeed might be very attractive for some institutional investors like insurance companies, as they promise a potential escape from the rising threats of the prevailing low-interest rate trap.

Furthermore, Solvency II as the new regulation regime for the European insurance industry also exerts a strong influence on the investment decisions of insurance companies, forcing them to generally narrow the industry´s typical duration gap. Since long-term sovereign bonds are currently not able to realize adequate returns, an investment in unlisted infrastructure equity can be a promising approach for realizing sufficient returns while contributing to a better duration matching of assets and liabilities.

However, resulting from the immaturity and heterogeneity of the entire infrastructure asset class in conjunction with the prevailing lack of market data, the current literature does not provide clear evidence about a generalized definition of infrastructure assets, their typical characteristics or their risk-return profiles on an aggregated level. Moreover, there is still a considerable uncertainty about the future shape of the infrastructure sector, particularly in the context of changing economic and social demands for infrastructure assets and the interdependency between public and private financing.

From an investor-oriented view, the performance of an insurance company´s portfolio investing in an usually illiquid asset like unlisted infrastructure equity, the asset´s contribution to the portfolio´s overall riskiness and the question of the portfolio´s optimal asset allocation under solvency requirements is not yet clear. With regard to regulatory policy, the appropriateness of the corresponding capital requirements to cover potential losses stemming from such infrastructure assets is still questionable.

Therefore, this book aims to shed some light on the appropriateness of the current regulatory treatment and the general suitability of unlisted infrastructure equity investments for the investment purposes of insurance companies. Due to the ongoing debates about this topic among supervisors, politicians, researchers and investors, the book comprises insights up to the middle of the year 2016. In the context of this publication, I want to thank everyone who supported me during my studies and the preparation of my master's thesis. I am particularly grateful to Prof. Dr. Helmut Gründl as the supervisor of my thesis and to the team of the International Center for Insurance Regulation (ICIR), whose research interest in insurance and insurance regulation made it possible for me to work on the important and contemporary topic of infrastructure investments in the insurance sector.

Table of Contents

List of Figures

List of Tables

List of Abbreviations

AnlV	Verordnung über die Anlage des Sicherungsvermögens von Pensionskassen, Sterbekassen und kleinen Versicherungsunternehmen (Anlageverordnung)
BSCR	Basic Solvency Capital Requirement
CAPM	Capital Asset Pricing Model
CIR	Cox-Ingersoll-Ross-model
DAX	Deutscher Aktienindex
DCF	Discounted Cash Flow
EEA	European Economic Area
EIOPA	European Insurance and Occupational Pensions Authority
GBM	Geometric Brownian Motion
GDP	Gross Domestic Product
LPE	Limited Purpose Entity
MCR	Minimum Capital Requirement
NPV	Net Present Value
OECD	Organisation for Economic Co-operation and Development
ORSA	Own Risk and Solvency Assessment
PPP	Public Private Partnership
PV	Present Value
QIS	Quantitative Impact Study
SCR	Solvency Capital Requirement
SDE	Stochastic Differential Equation
SPV	Special Purpose Vehicle
VaR	Value at Risk

1 Introduction

Infrastructure investments are frequently characterized as long-term investments generating stable cash flows, offering a good diversification potential as well as a sound protection against inflation. These attributes indeed might be very attractive for some institutional investors like insurance companies, as they promise a potential escape from the rising threats of the prevailing low-interest rate trap.

In this sense, the ongoing world-wide growth in the economic and social demand for well-functioning infrastructure assets leads currently to a global underfunding of the entire infrastructure sector of almost US $ 1 trillion per year. From a European perspective, it is expected that a cumulative capital demand for infrastructure investments of about EUR 1 trillion emerges until 2020. Due to tight public budgets remaining from the last financial crisis, and the risk that an underfinanced infrastructure sector can severely endanger an economy′s competitiveness and its ability to generate a high level of social welfare, governments are under strong pressure to continue or even to intensify the liberalization of the infrastructure sector, aiming to incentivize the capital market and its institutional investors to finance infrastructure projects.

Considering the recent developments, the insurance industry as the largest institutional investor in Europe has gradually shifted its investment focus towards this emerging segment, since it is considerably suffering from the prevailing low interest period. Especially life insurance companies in Germany are under strong pressure to realize sufficient returns in order to cover their large obligations resulting from the high guaranteed interest rates in the past. In addition, the new regulation regime for the European insurance industry, Solvency II, exerts a strong influence on the investment decisions of insurance companies. Its design generally prefers the narrowing of the industry′s typical duration gap, which in practice, is increasingly impeded by the prevailing low level of realizable yields not only for long-term sovereign bonds, but in a rising manner also for excellently rated corporates bonds, for instance, the recently issued bonds by Henkel or Sanofi-Aventis. In order to overcome this trap, a direct investment in infrastructure assets, for example the investment in a toll road or a power grid, can be a reasonable solution approach, because it allows the insurance company to directly benefit from the specific characteristics that are commonly perceived to be unique for infrastructure assets.

However, the adequate treatment of infrastructure assets in terms of their risk-return profiles for insurance companies, especially within the capital requirements imposed by the Solvency II framework, is still unclear and challenging. The ongoing debates show a distinct discrepancy between the different aims among supervisors, politicians, researchers and investors, regarding the infrastructure sector′s evolvement and its regulatory treatment in future. Therefore, this thesis aims to address some of the open issues and tries to contribute reasonable arguments for an objective debate.

1.1 Research questions

Resulting from the immaturity and heterogeneity of the entire infrastructure asset class in conjunction with the prevailing lack of market data, the current literature does not provide clear evidence about a generalized definition of infrastructure assets, their typical characteristics or risk-return profiles on an aggregated level. In addition, there is still a considerable uncertainty about the future shape of the infrastructure sector, particularly in the context of changing economic and social demands for infrastructure assets and the interdependency between public and private financing. However, the findings of the emerging scientific research over the last decade allows to draw first conclusions on these open issues when considering only specific asset sub-classes. Since direct infrastructure assets as an individual sub-class are increasingly subject to the investment purposes of institutional investors like insurance companies, they seem to provide a promising topic for this thesis.

From the perspective of an insurance company, a direct investment in an infrastructure asset, for example, the investment or the financing of the unlisted equity stake of physical assets like toll roads or power grids, is commonly perceived to be a valuable investment opportunity, at least if the asset behaves in a stylized manner. This type of sub-class exhibits the closest relation to the infrastructure business model of all asset classes currently available on the capital market and hence allows for the strongest exploitation of the specific characteristics that differentiate infrastructure assets from any other assets.

The performance of an insurance company´s portfolio investing in an usually illiquid asset like unlisted infrastructure equity, the asset´s contribution to the portfolio´s overall riskiness and the question of the portfolio´s optimal asset allocation under solvency requirements is not yet clear. The need of addressing these issues gains in importance against the background that they have not been subject to the literature so far and are thus offering a promising field of research.

In addition, the appropriateness of the corresponding regulatory capital requirements to cover potential losses stemming from such infrastructure assets is still questionable. Despite the recent changes under the standard formula of Solvency II, its current design and intention to determine these capital requirements seem to be unnecessarily complex and might evolve as a hindering factor for the future emergence of the infrastructure sector. Thus, the right treatment of direct infrastructure assets is still issue of ongoing debates among supervisors, politicians, researchers and investors, but all of them exhibiting different opinions to some extent.

Consequently, there is a need for a more detailed research on direct infrastructure assets. This thesis aims to address the following five research questions (RQ) in order to shed some light on the appropriateness of the current regulatory treatment and the general suitability of direct infrastructure assets for the investment purposes of an insurance company.

<u>RQ1a:</u> What is the current status of the infrastructure market, which opportunities of investing in infrastructure assets are currently available and how can they be classified?

<u>RQ1b:</u> What are the current insights about the performance and the riskiness of a direct infrastructure asset and is it generally suitable for investment purposes of insurance companies?

RQ2: How are direct infrastructure assets currently treated under Solvency II and to what extent is it prudentially justified?

RQ3: How can such an asset be modelled for simulation purposes, especially to reflect the specificity of its risk-return profile, in order to be consistent with a market oriented, true and fair-view valuation?

RQ4: How do the performance and the riskiness of an insurance company's portfolio investing in an infrastructure asset evolve over time? How do the portfolio's solvency capital requirements based on the VaR approach and on the standard formula behave?

RQ5: What is a potentially more appropriate capital charge for the underlying infrastructure asset under the standard formula of Solvency II?

1.2 Research approach

The research questions RQ1, RQ2 and RQ3 are mainly addressed by means of a qualitative analysis of the currently vast stream of literature regarding the area of infrastructure assets. Thereby, the findings primarily inferred by academic literature and to some extent by business reports are taken into account. The research questions RQ4 and RQ5 are examined by means of a quantitative analysis using a Monte Carlo simulation.

The thesis is organized as follows. Chapter 2 provides a comprehensive overview of the findings in literature regarding the current status of the entire infrastructure sector (RQ1a). It aims to identify its market potential for private investors by clarifying superior trends that are commonly expected to shape the demand for infrastructure investments in future. Due to the plurality of classification schemes for infrastructure assets in the literature, it consolidates the most important classification characteristics in order to provide a comprehensive overview of the current infrastructure sector and its fragmentation.

Furthermore, the chapter identifies the major risk sources that are common to direct infrastructure assets and connects them to the typical lifecycle of such assets. Thus, it enables to attain general insights about the time-variant change of the underlying risk profile of infrastructure assets. Finally, the chapter ends by presenting the empirical results regarding the risk-return profiles found in literature and draws several concluding remarks about the asset's appropriateness for an investment by insurance companies (RQ1b).

Chapter 3 covers the ongoing debate about the adequate regulatory treatment of direct infrastructure assets by pointing out the recent changes in the regulatory regime under Solvency II (RQ2). Therefore, it clarifies the current opportunities for insurance companies to determine the solvency capital requirement of such an asset under the standard formula and assesses its appropriateness critically. Furthermore, it highlights a general discrepancy in the treatment of the equity and interest rate risk for infrastructure assets.

The subsequent chapter 4 comprises the remaining research questions RQ3, RQ4 and RQ5. In order to perform the quantitative analysis of these questions, the theoretical foundation of a valuation model for the infrastructure asset by means of a discounted cash flow approach is set up and evaluated in section 4.1 (RQ3). Thereby, it reflects the main results regarding the asset´s common risk-return profile previously addressed by RQ1b.

For assessing the performance and riskiness of an insurance company´s portfolio investing in an infrastructure asset (RQ4), the evolution of an entire balance sheet over time is modeled by means of a Monte Carlo simulation. The balance sheet basically comprises stochastic processes for a risk-free asset, a risky asset, the infrastructure asset and the liabilities (section 4.2). Thereby, the insurance company aims to maximize its net shareholder value as an objective function while it is subject to specific constraints (section 4.3). Based on the optimized portfolio´s composition, the rationale behind the infrastructure asset´s influence on the insurance company´s choice of the optimal portfolio weights is analyzed. Furthermore, a sensitivity analysis is conducted in order to infer the asset´s general dynamics within the portfolio.

Finally, the solvency capital requirements are determined by the application of a VaR approach and the standard formula of Solvency II. Due to the mismatch in the amounts of both capital requirements, section 4.4 aims to determine a potentially more appropriate capital charge for the underlying infrastructure asset under the standard formula by means of a VaR approach (RQ5).

In chapter 5, the quantitative results are critically discussed with a focus on the most important aspects and by considering the obtained results of the qualitative analysis. Furthermore, it suggests several starting points to improve the overall quality of the results in further research. Chapter 6 finally provides concluding remarks.

2 Overview of the infrastructure asset class

Despite the lack of a unique definition of infrastructure assets, its overall asset class principally comprises physical structures and networks that facilitate basic services for the existence, competitiveness and further development of both, an economy and a society.[1] It is often claimed that the ideal infrastructure investment generates predictable, long-term and stable cash flows that show a low correlation with other investments available on the capital market, protects against inflation risk and exhibits some kind of monopolistic market characteristics.[2] These properties, if existing in practice, appear to be the desired salvation for institutional investors like insurance companies, as they mitigate the jeopardy of the prevailing low-interest rate period. In order to capture that potential, the following sections shed some light on the typical characteristics that infrastructure investments tend to have in common and clarify the resulting consequences for their underlying risk-return profiles.

2.1 Current market situation for infrastructure investments

There is some evidence in the literature that in general, increasing infrastructure expenditures exert a positive influence on an economy´s future growth, especially towards the long run.[3] In this sense, the World Economic Forum (2012) estimates that every dollar spent on functional, i.e. value adding, public infrastructure will generate an economic return of five to 25 % in terms of gross domestic product (GDP) growth.[4] Although this interdependence between economic growth and infrastructure expenditures might act to some extent as a driving force for governmental spending in the infrastructure sector, there is still a large unmet capital demand for infrastructure investments around the world, leading to a global infrastructure gap of almost US $ 1 trillion per year.[5] The literature offers a vast variety of different figures on the right capital endowment for the entire infrastructure sector, but altogether, they finally draw the picture of a severe discrepancy between the capital´s provision and demand. The OECD (2007) forecasts that there is a global, cumulative capital need of about US $ 70 trillion until 2030 only for the publically most important sectors transport, communication, energy and water.[6] McKinsey Global Institute (2013) estimates a world-wide capital requirement of about US $ 57 trillion for the same sectors only to keep up with the current expectations of economic growth until 2030.[7] With regard to Europe, the European Commission (2014) estimates a cumulative capital demand for infrastructure investments in the fields of transport, energy and communication of about EUR 1 trillion until 2020.[8] Considering the amount of expected

---

[1] See Newell/Peng (2008), p. 22; OECD (2007), p. 20; WEF (2012), pp. 2-3.

[2] See, amongst others, Inderst (2010), p. 73.

[3] See Sanchez-Robles (1998), p. 106; Esfahani/Ramirez (2003), pp. 470-471; Canning/Pedroni (2008), pp. 523-524.

[4] See WEF (2012), p. 2.

[5] Measured as the difference between capital need and spending, see WEF (2012), p. 1.

[6] See OECD (2007), p. 97.

[7] See McKinsey Global Institute (2013), p. 1.

[8] See European Commission (2014), p. 2.

infrastructure spending, PwC (2014) forecasts a global rise of yearly capital expenditures for infrastructure assets from US $ 4 trillion in 2012 to US $ 9 trillion by 2025.[9]

Although all of these figures should be treated as rough estimates depending on many different economic scenarios, they all have the expectation of an enormous capital demand for future infrastructure investments in common. This expectation can be further supported by four long-term trends that seem to exert a major influence on the future deployment of the global infrastructure needs and thus provide valuable investment opportunities for institutional investors like insurance companies.[10]

First, there are fundamentally demographic developments in effect which basically evolve from two distinctions, population growth and population ageing.[11] From the perspective of the infrastructure sector, a growing and ageing population inevitably requires two capital-intensive actions, on the one hand, to intensely increase the existing infrastructure capacities and on the other hand, to build additional ones in order to satisfy the changing needs of the total population. The pressure stemming from these distinctions can be severe, as for instance, it is expected that until 2030 about 16 % of the worldwide population will be aged 60 years or over, while this group accounts for even more than 25 % of total population in Europe.[12] Resulting from a growing proportion of the old-aged people among societies, this trend is likely to emerge as a tightening condition on public budgets, leading through higher social expenses to an accelerating decline in remaining public funds for future infrastructure spending. In 2014, the average proportion of public social expenditures across the OECD countries already reached a historically high level with about 21.6 % of the GDP.[13] Since the public expenditures for pensions and social welfare are commonly expected to grow for most developed countries, it is likely that this trend will retain to shrink public funds available for infrastructure investments and thus, a growing participation of private investors like insurance companies in financing infrastructure assets seems to be inevitable.

Furthermore, as a result of the recent financial and sovereign debt crises, severe financial constraints on public budgets of both, developed and emerging countries, have been imposed in a widely manner. These come into effect, for example, through national debt brakes like they are implemented in Germany or through higher yield spreads of sovereign bonds, in particularly for highly indebted countries like Greece.[14] Therefore, governments around the world are under strong pressure to reduce their public debt levels and to consolidate their budgets.[15] In case of the European Union, the average gross debt level relative to GDP raised from 61.3 % in 2004

[9] See PwC (2014), p. 6-7.

[10] See, amongst others, OECD (2007), p. 21; PwC (2014), pp. 14-19.

[11] See OECD (2007), pp. 155-157.

[12] See United Nations (2015), p. 3.

[13] See OECD (2016a), statistics about social expenditure.

[14] See Bundesbank (2014), p. 26 for the development of bond spreads.

[15] A good example is Greece and its long-term struggle against the debt burden.

up to 85.2 % in 2015,[16] leading to average interest payments of about 2.3 % of the GDP.[17] In this regard, Checherita-Westphal and Rother (2012) show that the influence of high public debt levels on both, the long-term economic growth as well as the governmental investment behavior, is negative and non-linear.[18] Although there is currently some debt relief through the low interest rate environment for some countries like Germany, the generally increasing public debt levels in conjunction with a higher social spending are rather likely to negatively affect the available public expenditures for infrastructure investments in future and can be seen as the second major trend for a stronger involvement of private investors.

With regard to the long-term economic growth, for which a well-funded infrastructure sector is clearly a precondition, PwC (2015) estimates a significant change in the global economic order in terms of national GDP values from the current G7 (USA, Japan, Germany, United Kingdom, France, Italy, Canada) to a new group of emerging economies, called E7 (China, India, Brazil, Russia, Indonesia, Mexico, Turkey) in 2050.[19] Measured at purchasing power parity, the cumulative GDP of the E7 is expected to be twice that of the G7, whereof based on its national contributions, China and India are on first and second rank, followed by the USA.[20] This forecast can be underpinned by academic literature, for example, Jorgenson and Vu (2013), who point out a similar change in the global economic order until 2020.[21] Therefore, the emerging economies are expected to account for about half of global infrastructure expenditures over the next decades and hence generate an enormous capital demand for financing infrastructure assets.[22] In combination with constrained public budgets even in these countries, the covering of this capital need is likely to offer a wide variety of valuable investment opportunities for insurance companies and builds the third trend.

The last major trend can be found in a growing public sensitivity to the environmental status. For the infrastructure sector, this sensitivity implies a need for action not only limited to a reduction of environmental pollution caused by the infrastructure systems, but also for increasing the resilience of existing infrastructure assets to adverse natural outcomes and disasters.[23] Hence, it is likely that the current shift in the investment focus of several major institutional investors towards environmental issues will continue in future and tie their investments more strongly to an environmental context.[24] This expectation can be supported, for instance, by the growing effort of Scandinavian funds for divestment in polluting infrastructure assets or by data provided by Preqin (2016a), showing that the majority of global

---

[16] See Eurostat (2016a), statistics about general government gross debt.

[17] See Eurostat (2016b), statistics about general government gross debt w.r.t. interest payable.

[18] See Checherita-Westphal/Rother (2012), p. 1403.

[19] See PwC (2015), pp. 8-10.

[20] See PwC (2015), p 3.

[21] See Jorgenson/Vu (2013), pp. 398-399.

[22] See McKinsey Global Institute (2013), p. 23.

[23] See McKinsey Global Institute (2013), p. 17.

[24] See OECD (2007), pp. 162-167.

infrastructure deals over the last few years has already been completed in the field of renewable energy.[25]

These four superior trends are commonly expected to strongly challenge the future evolvement of infrastructure investments.[26] Since a government´s ability of financing infrastructure investments through taxation is limited, it is inevitable for governments in future to increase the privatization among public infrastructure assets, liberalize the structures of the infrastructure market and to incentivize private investors to meet these four long-term challenges under governmental supervision. As stated by the OECD (2007) and by Kikeri and Nellis (2004), governments basically need to change their future role from an exclusive investor in infrastructure towards a prudent supervisor who sets up attractive financing conditions for private investors and only stipulates the major aims under which private investors fund infrastructure assets.[27]

In this regard, there is already an increasing political effort to incentivize capital markets for financing infrastructure investments, for instance, through the introduction of the Europe 2020 Project Bond Initiative starting in 2012 by the European Union that aims to foster infrastructure debt investments.[28] Despite these first public programs, the current market for infrastructure assets cannot be seen as established, since private investors willing to fund infrastructure investments lack a standardized access to the various types of infrastructure investments. In order to overcome this obstacle, there are first efforts for a generalization of single market segments emerging in the literature. The extensive review of this literature stream has pointed out that there are three different main approaches commonly used to categorize the currently extremely heterogeneous infrastructure asset class into several major asset sub-classes. Every approach emphasizes different characteristics and risks of the underlying infra-structure asset, but if considered together, as intended in this thesis, these approaches are expected to provide a comprehensive overview of the infrastructure market´s current fragmentation.

The first approach categorizes infrastructure investments by the field of their operating business sector (sector approach). This perspective distinguishes between economic infrastructure assets, meaning physical systems that enable the basic functioning of the economy and society, and social infrastructure assets, which refer to systems and institutions that provide services essential for the continuity of a society (see Table 1). The field of economic infrastructure mainly includes the sectors transport, utilities and communication, whereas social infrastructure comprises the sectors health, education, security, culture, administration and retirement. Potential investors need to consider at first the suitability of the preferred business sector for their investment purposes, since all sectors can differentiate heavily in terms of, for example, risk sources, market competition or geopolitical factors that ultimately affect the investment´s expected return. Thus, it is difficult to draw a general conclusion about the eligibility of individual sectors, but, because investments in social infrastructure are usually subject to severe constraints, for example, in terms of a regulatory return cap or a compulsion for regularly capital

[25] See The Guardian (2016) and Preqin (2016a), p. 1.

[26] See e.g. OECD (2007), p. 14.

[27] See OECD (2007), pp. 30-31 and Kikeri/Nellis (2004), pp. 113-114.

[28] See European Union (2012), Regulation No 670/2012.

injections by the investor, infrastructure assets among this sector might be rather inappropriate for insurance companies.

Table 1: Infrastructure categorization using the sector approach

<table>
<tr><th colspan="3">Economic infrastructure</th><th colspan="3">Social infrastructure</th></tr>
<tr><td rowspan="2"><u>Transport</u>

- Ground:
Roads, Rails, Bridges, Public transport
- Water:
Ports, Water routes
- Air:
Airports</td><td rowspan="2"><u>Utilities</u>

- Energy, Water, Heat supply:
Oil, Gas, Coal, Renewable energy sources
- Energy distribution:
Power grids, Energy storage
- Waste management</td><td rowspan="2"><u>Communication</u>

- Cable networks
- Satellites
- Radio stations</td><td><u>Health</u>

- Hos-pitals</td><td><u>Education</u>

- Schools, Universities</td><td><u>Security</u>

- Prisons, Police</td></tr>
<tr><td><u>Culture</u>

- Parks
- Sports buildings</td><td><u>Administration</u>

- Adminis-trative buildings
- Courts</td><td><u>Retire-ment</u>

- Retire-ment homes</td></tr>
</table>

Source: Own table, based on Gatzert/Kosub (2014), p. 353 and Kleine/Krautbauer/Schulz (2015), p. 81.

The second approach separates infrastructure investments according to their maturity (investment stage approach). Infrastructure investments at an early stage are commonly considered as greenfield assets, whereas investments at a later stage as brownfield assets.[29] This separation can be seen as a first risk-sensitive classification of infrastructure investments, because it differentiates the asset´s risk exposure depending on its stage on the lifecycle, which can be usually divided into four separate phases. At first, a design and planning phase builds the technical foundation for every infrastructure asset, which is followed by a capital-intensive construction phase in order to enable the investor with the ability to realize cash flows during the operating phase. The end of this lifecycle is usually represented by a decommissioning phase, during which the asset usually loses heavily in value due to fewer remaining operating periods and higher maintenance costs.[30]

Comparing greenfield to brownfield assets, the former type of asset does either not exist or only stands at an early project stage, so that it still needs to be constructed, which typically adds a plenty of additional risk sources to those mandatory for the operating phase.[31] Brownfield assets usually refer to assets that are already established and generate cash flows, hence they do not include any design and planning or construction risks and can provide more information for potential investors in terms of, for example, demand patterns about the asset´s underlying business model, insights about the market dynamics or its regulation.[32] Therefore, the asset´s

[29] See Oyedele/Adair/McGreal (2014), pp. 3-4.

[30] See Gatzert/Kosub (2014), p. 353; Ehlers (2014), p. 5.

[31] See Oyedele/Adair/McGreal (2014), pp. 3-4.

[32] See Bitsch/Buchner/Kaserer (2010), p. 112.

lifecycle status as a distinctive feature highlights brownfield assets as less risky than greenfield assets, but in turn, they also realize lower returns for the investor.[33] From the perspective of an insurance company as a risk-averse investor, brownfield assets seem to be a rather suitable investment choice, since the recent history provides good examples for the financial jeopardy of the greenfield assets´ construction phase (e.g. the Berlin airport).

The third categorization approach of infrastructure investments is based on the final investment vehicle that is used for the investor´s acquisition process (Table 2, investment vehicle approach).[34] Considering the scattered insights among the literature, it seems to be useful to subsume these by a three-step approach in order to illustrate the complexity of the investor´s current decision process for financing an infrastructure asset. At first, there is the investor´s basic distinction between an equity or debt investment in the preferred infrastructure sector (capital type), for example, the investment in stocks or bonds, which is followed by the choice of a preferred degree of the investor´s own influence on the asset (investment type), for instance, a direct or indirect investment through funds, and as the final step, there is the selection of the preferred degree of standardization underlying the acquisition process, for example, buying the targeted combination of capital and investment type as a listed or unlisted asset (investment vehicle).

Due to the extreme complexity of this three-step approach, it is not possible to conclude a general eligibility of any combination over the others for insurance companies (Table 2). All of them exhibit different characteristics, especially in terms of their risk and return contribution to the investor´s portfolio or the underlying market depth, leading to the intense heterogeneity of the infrastructure asset class at an aggregated level. But it clarifies the current challenges an investor is subject to when deciding on financing infrastructure, which, altogether, require a deep understanding of the infrastructure market and its complex dynamics. Therefore, the following section explains each investment vehicle in greater detail in order to comprehend and assess some of these issues.

33 See Oyedele/Adair/McGreal (2014), pp. 3-4 and Bitsch/Buchner/Kaserer (2010), p. 123.

34 See, for example, Gatzert/Kosub (2014), pp. 354-358.

Table 2: Infrastructure categorization using the investment vehicle approach (Part I)

Capital Type	Vehicle / Type	Listed Asset	Unlisted Asset
Equity	Direct	<u>Stocks:</u> • Market depth: Deep capital markets available • Liquidity: High • Know-how requirement: Capital market know-how • Diversification potential: Low, usually high correlation with other equity assets in the market	<u>Unlisted equities / PPPs:</u> • Market depth: Limited opportunities • Liquidity: Low, usually less exit options • Know-how requirement: High, specific project and business model know-how • Diversification potential: Rather high due to stable cash flows
	Indirect	<u>Listed equity funds:</u> • Market depth: Limited market • Liquidity: Medium • Know-how requirement: Capital market know-how • Diversification potential: Low, usually high correlation of the fund´s portfolio with other equity assets	<u>Unlisted equity funds:</u> • Market depth: Limited market • Liquidity: Low to medium • Know-how requirement: High, specific sector and business model know-how • Diversification potential: Basically, rather high level, but depending on assets´ sectors and regions

Table 2: Infrastructure categorization using the investment vehicle approach (Part II)

Capital Type	Vehicle / Type	Listed Asset	Unlisted Asset
Debt	Direct	Corporate Bonds: • Market depth: Limited capital market • Liquidity: High • Know-how requirement: Fixed-Income and business model know-how • Diversification potential: Rather low, usually high correlation with other bonds in the market	Project Loans / Project Bonds: • Market depth: High supply, but mainly dominated by banks • Liquidity: Low, no secondary market yet • Know-how requirement: Credit market and business know-how • Diversification potential: Rather high due to direct link to stable infrastructure business models
	Indirect	Bond funds / Loan funds: For this segment, there are only few market offers available (around 40 funds in 2012) which do not provide sufficient track records and data for proper performance assessment according to the literature.	

Source: Own table, based on Gatzert/Kosub (2014), pp. 354-358; Kleine/Krautbauer/Schulz (2012), pp. 27-28, pp. 58-60; Bitsch/Buchner/Kaserer (2010), pp. 109-110.

For the field of direct equity investments, the investor can basically choose between an investment in a listed equity stake of a company whose business model is related to the infrastructure sector or an investment in an unlisted and hence private equity stake of an infrastructure company or physical asset. The former type of asset relates to publically traded stocks which are usually relatively liquid, require only profound capital market knowledge and their performance is usually correlated to a certain degree with the overall market performance.[35] Therefore, the properties of this asset sub-class are relatively similar to those of other listed equities. The latter one comprises direct capital investments in physical assets such as, for instance, toll roads, power plants or power grids, which can be acquired and managed by investors on their own behalf or in share with a government in case of a more specific investment structure like a public private partnership (PPP).

PPPs are characterized by a certain form of cooperation between a private investor (often bearing the design, planning and construction risk) and the government (often bearing the demand, pricing and inflation risk) which is contractually arranged for a certain length of time.[36]

[35] See Bitsch/Buchner/Kaserer (2010), p. 109.

[36] See OECD (2007), p 32; for a comprehensive overview see Grimsey/Lewis (2002).

A well-negotiated PPP can be advantageous for both parties, the private investor who mitigates some specific risk factors to the public partner, and the government which can reduce its public expenditures for infrastructure. However, it is not possible to generalize the economic performance of PPP structures, because it highly depends on the exact risk allocation and tariff structure between both parties underlying each deal.[37]

In general, direct investments in unlisted infrastructure equity as an individual sub asset-class are usually characterized by the requirement of large capital commitments as well as a profound knowledge about the assets' underlying business models and its sectors.[38] In addition, the commitments usually underlie long time horizons accompanied by only a few possible exit options for investors, which characterizes the investment as rather illiquid and to be more risky compared to their listed or indirect counterparts within the infrastructure market.[39] However, due to their direct relation to infrastructure business models, which is shown by Bitsch (2012) to generally provide more stable cash flows than non-infrastructure business models, these investments can be considered as rather eligible for portfolio diversification purposes.[40]

Indirect equity investments through the investor's participation in a public or private fund investing in either listed or unlisted infrastructure equity stakes, represent an alternative approach for even smaller investors to engage in the field of infrastructure. The main motives for investors to select this type of investment are, for instance, to participate in the relatively stable infrastructure business models while providing an usually lower capital commitment than for direct investments, a lower degree of own asset management duties as investors often act as limited fund partners and finally, to be endowed with several, standardized exit options depending on the fund's legal framework (e.g. regulated withdrawal of money, sale of partnership to a secondary investor etc.).[41] The diversification potential of this type of asset for institutional investors like insurance companies depends highly on the regionally and sector-specifically clustering of infrastructure investments within the fund's portfolio, but can be considered as relatively advantageous in contrast to other types of investments on the capital market.[42]

In case of debt investments, the market currently offers only direct investments to a sufficient extent.[43] These can be split between either listed debt assets, for example, listed bonds of companies associated with the infrastructure business, or unlisted debt assets, for instance, direct loans or bonds for certain infrastructure projects. It is reported that listed corporate infrastructure bonds behave rather similar to bonds from non-infrastructure companies in terms

[37] For typical PPP contracts in practice, see for example Blanc-Brude (2013), pp. 19-20 and Zhang (2005), p. 657.

[38] See, e.g. Bitsch/Buchner/Kaserer (2010), p. 109.

[39] See Gatzert/Kosub (2014), p. 354; Finkenzeller/Dechant/Schäfers (2010), p. 266.

[40] See Bitsch (2012), p. 209; Kleine/Krautbauer/Schulz (2012), p. 59.

[41] See Bitsch/Buchner/Kaserer (2010), p. 109.

[42] See Gatzert/Kosub (2014), p. 354.

[43] See Kleine/Krautbauer/Schulz (2012), p. 55.

of risk-return when having the same credit rating and maturity, thus offering a low exploitation of the potential benefits of the infrastructure business.[44]

Infrastructure loans in contrast, provide a direct access to infrastructure business models. Regarding the average cumulative default rates of infrastructure project loans, which measure the probability of a cohort´s default up to distinct time intervals, these seem not to entirely reflect the stylized potential of infrastructure assets in terms of cash flows´ stability and riskiness. Based on recent data and rating categories from Moody's, such infrastructure loans are classified in a range between low to speculative investment grade (Moody´s Baa/Ba rating).[45] In contrast, considering the marginal annual default rates, which measure the probability that a member of a cohort which has survived up to a specific date will default by the end of that time interval, infrastructure loans seem to reflect the stylized potential of infrastructure assets only after a certain period of time. Starting with the high levels of non-investment grade´s marginal annual default rates, the rates for infrastructure loans fall three years after their closing towards those consistent with upper investment grade loans (Moody´s A rating).[46] The relatively high marginal default rates at the beginning of the infrastructure loan´s settlement compared to their later values are likely to result from the general high riskiness of the infrastructure asset´s underlying construction phase, for which the history provides several examples (e.g. the Berlin airport).[47]

This comprehensive overview shows that the market for infrastructure investments offers a plenty of different opportunities for investors to engage in the field of infrastructure. Recent data highlights that among institutional investors, insurance companies are currently the fourth largest investor in infrastructure.[48] However, regarding their average target aim for their portfolios´ allocation to infrastructure assets (3.9 %), it deviates significantly from their current portfolio´s exposure (2.9 %).[49] One rationale behind this mismatch can be found in the still unclear evidence on the empirical performance and riskiness of infrastructure investments, thus, resulting in a challenging valuation processes, which is stated to be one of the major problematic market issues institutional investors are concerned about.[50] This is not surprising, since there is a common complaint among practitioners as well as researchers about the prevailing lack of sufficient market data for infrastructure investments in order to properly assess their true risk-return profiles.[51]

This thesis will focus on direct investments in unlisted infrastructure equity stakes (hereafter named as direct infrastructure assets) from the perspective of an insurance company, because

[44] See Kleine/Krautbauer/Schulz (2012), p. 49.

[45] See Moody´s (2013), p. 16 and Moody´s (2011), p. 33.

[46] See Moody´s (2013), p. 18.

[47] See Moody´s (2013), p. 18.

[48] See Preqin (2016b), p. 35.

[49] See Preqin (2016b), p. 36.

[50] See Preqin (2016b), p. 38.

[51] See e.g. Bahceci/Weisdorf (2014), p. 1.

this type of investment offers the strongest potential to participate in the special properties that tend to be unique for infrastructure assets. Therefore, this asset class is expected to represent the currently most valuable investment opportunity for insurance companies in the field of infrastructure assets. The following section provides scientific results in order to quantify their market potential as well as their risk-return profiles and hence builds the foundation for an own valuation model of an infrastructure asset developed in chapter 4.

2.2 The risk-return profile of direct infrastructure assets

It can be generally advantageous for institutional investors like insurance companies to directly invest in unlisted infrastructure equity and hence own this position in their balance sheets. According to the literature, direct infrastructure assets, at least in a stylized manner, are perceived to exhibit features like, for instance, high hurdles for a competitor's market entry in terms of capital and business knowledge requirements, a generally long business model duration, a low correlation of the assets' returns with other asset classes, an inelastic market demand pattern for the assets' underlying business models which provides the ability for a sound inflation hedge and finally, relatively low default rates.[52] Furthermore, it is also frequently claimed that such infrastructure investments depict some kind of a hybrid asset, because one the one hand, they tend to combine equity-like returns with bond-like risks and on the other hand, they show some similarity to real estate investments.[53]

Although there are infrastructure investments that seem to satisfy some of these stylized features quite well, for instance the renewable energy sector in Germany with its feed-in tariff, a generalization of these features to hold for the entire infrastructure asset class is currently either not possible or at least challenging due to the prevailing lack of independent market data and the scarcity of empirical literature regarding the performance of infrastructure investments.[54] Nevertheless, academic research has identified several diverse risk sources that tend to be typically apparent for direct infrastructure assets and thus, build a suitable starting point for the assessment of its general risk-return profile.[55] However, the impact of these risk sources on an asset's total performance can be highly diverse and differs strongly from investment to investment, since Tables 1 and 2 indicate the high heterogeneity of the whole infrastructure asset class. In order to comprehend the main risk channels underlying all direct infrastructure assets, Table 3 aims to aggregate the common risk sources found in literature to the typical lifecycle stages of such an infrastructure investment.[56] By connecting the risk sources to the different time-variant stages, it is possible to draw a first conclusion about the general distribution of risks among the total lifetime of such an asset and hence to provide the theoretical foundation for modelling the infrastructure asset in chapter 4.

---

[52] See Inderst (2010), p. 73; Peng/Newell (2007), p. 424; See Moody's (2013), p. 18.

[53] See Inderst (2010), p. 78; Newell/Peng (2008), p. 25.

[54] Private databases mostly used are provided by Preqin, Mercer Investment Consulting or CEPRES.

[55] For a comprehensive overview of risks, see, e.g. Inderst (2010), pp. 80-81; Loosemore (2007), p. 71; Bing et al. (2005), p. 28.

[56] Typical lifecycles mentioned by, e.g., Ehlers (2014), p. 5.

During the design and planning phase, which typically marks the first phase in the lifespan of an infrastructure asset, especially site and technical risks seem to appear. Common sources of risk can be found in challenges with land use and ground condition (e.g. in terms of suitability for the infrastructure project, its consistence, ground pollution, animal and plant protection, etc.) or design failures (e.g. in terms of inefficient technical solutions to specific problems emerging in subsequent stages).[57] In order to avoid a significant delay of the remaining lifecycle phases, high effort should be allocated by investors to the analysis of the risks involved at this project stage. Significant failures are even more dangerous to the asset´s total realization, since infrastructure investments are usually subject to a J-curve effect of cash flows, which means that the asset is not able to generate cash flows to cover any unexpected incoming expenditures.[58] The case of the Berlin airport and its problems with the smoke extraction system is a good example for the magnitude and tediousness of failures during this stage on the asset´s overall evolvement and the scope of necessary capital injections made by investors.

The probably most dangerous risk sources seem to appear during the asset´s construction phase, since any cost overruns during this stage cannot be compensated by operating cash flows and the termination of the entire construction project is mostly rather capital-intensive. Typical risk sources according to the literature include site risks, financial risks, regulatory or political risks, cost overruns and delays in the completion of the construction. All of these aggregated sources emerge in a plenty of different and individual risk factors which vary in their impact on the construction phase´s risk contribution to the asset´s total performance. Resulting from the strong relation between the construction risk and the default risk of infrastructure loans as data provided by Moody´s (2013) highlight, the construction phase can be regarded as a significant influence factor for the overall success of the infrastructure asset and thus should be considered carefully by potential investors and emphasized when modeling infrastructure assets.[59]

Considering the operation phase, the infrastructure asset during this stage typically generates first cash flows that are able to compensate the major risk sources appearing at this stage, like financial risks, regulatory or political risks, business risks and environmental risks. During this phase, regulatory and political risks might have the most disruptive potential to the asset´s business model depending on its underlying degree of regulation.[60] Recent history points out how dangerous this threat can be to the total performance of entire infrastructure sectors that were formerly perceived to be stable and profitable, for instance, the changes in the renewable energy market in Spain in 2014 or Germany´s nuclear power market due to its phase-out of nuclear power plants after the incidents in Fukushima in 2011.[61] It is obviously that the magnitude of negative consequences caused by regulatory changes increases with a higher degree of the business model´s regulatory level. Even if this risk type is difficult to mitigate, investors should be aware of its disruptive potential and try to reduce its magnitude as most as

[57] The sources for the arguments regarding the lifecycle stages are mainly provided under Table 3 for the sake of comprehensiveness.

[58] See Gatzert/Kosub (2014), p. 353.

[59] See Moody´s (2013), p. 18; The sources for the arguments regarding the lifecycle stages are mainly provided under Table 3.

[60] Preqin (2016b) highlights on p. 38 the field of regulation as one of the major issues for the infrastructure market.

[61] For a comprehensive overview of the Spanish renewable energy market see Rojas/Tubio (2015).

possible, for instance, by negotiating suitably contractual frameworks in case of public private partnerships.

Table 3: Major risk factors for direct infrastructure assets (Part I)

Phase	Type of risk	Source of risk	Impact
Design and Planning	Site risks	Land use, ground condition issues like suitability, pollution, animal and plant protection, etc.	This risk can reach a high level and even lead to project termination in case of, e.g. unsolved environment protection conflicts, etc.
	Technical risks	Design failure, etc.	Inefficient technical solutions to issues of the subsequent stages can have extreme financial consequences, e.g. new Berlin airport.
Construction	Site risks	See above, but unexperienced in the design and planning phase.	See above.
	Financial risks	Interest rate shift, inflation rate changes, exchange rate shift, leverage risks, etc.	Financial risks during the construction phase can affect solvency of both, the investor as well as the construction contractor.
	Cost overruns	Design failures, approval delays, material price changes, etc.	A correction of fundamental design failures can be effort-extensive and expensive. A delay of required approvals at this stage can delay the completion of the whole construction phase.
	Regulatory/ Political Risks	Approval delays, changes in law affecting the conditions of the construction or the operating phases, etc.	It can require new design elements and delay the whole construction phase. Further, it can even make the intended business model inefficient.
	Delay in completion	Approval delays, inefficient work management, etc.	This risk can lead to high opportunity costs in terms of unmet demand.

Table 3: Major risk factors for direct infrastructure assets (Part II)

Phase	Type of risk	Source of risk	Impact
Operating	Financial risks	See above.	These risks can lead to severe financial distress during operation phase.
	Regulatory/ Political risks	See above, plus risk of tariff changes, market liberalization, etc.	Tariff changes can endanger the total business model, e.g. renewable energy market in Spain in 2014.
	Business risks	Operating cost overruns, revenue risk (demand, pricing risk), tax changes, agency conflicts between investor and government, etc.	These factors can significantly affect the total performance of the business model. Especially demand risk can be severe, e.g. the phase-out of nuclear energy in Germany in 2011.
	Environmental risks	Natural disaster, pollution, waste, etc.	Environmental risk can be caused by infrastructure projects or these can be physically affected by natural disasters.
Decommissioning	Illiquidity risks	Less exit options.	There is no secondary market for infrastructure projects, hence it is difficult to find a subsequent investor.
	Pricing/ Valuation risks	Difficulties with valuation of salvage value due to uncertainty in future political/regulatory environment.	It can be very problematic to value a project if there is uncertainty regarding the political/regulatory environment.

Source: Own table, based on EY (2015), pp. 18-20; Inderst (2010), pp. 80-81; Loosemore (2007), p. 71; Bing et al. (2005), p. 28.

The decommissioning phase usually refers to risk types such as illiquidity and valuation risks that on the one hand, also arise during the whole lifespan of an infrastructure investment, but remain as a more adverse characteristic at the asset´s final lifecycle´s phase when its market value usually shrinks caused by fewer operating periods. Due to the absence of a secondary market for direct infrastructure assets, there are only few feasible exit options for investors resulting in a high illiquidity risk.[62] This in turn, contributes to the lack of market data of comparable assets and transactions, which further complicates the valuation process of infrastructure assets, especially if there is uncertainty about major risk factors like political or

[62] See, e.g. Finkenzeller/Dechant/Schäfers (2010), p. 266 or Inderst (2010), p. 80; The sources for the arguments regarding the lifecycle stages are mainly provided under Table 3.

regulatory risk in future. This might work as an additional pressure for investors to hold such illiquid assets until maturity. However, on the other hand, especially the illiquidity risk can be in turn a valuable aspect for long-term investors like insurance companies, which are able to skim an underlying illiquidity premium compared to rather short-term investors.

Although every infrastructure investment is faced with most of these risks, their occurrence and their precise influence on the asset´s overall performance can highly differ from asset to asset depending on many diverse aspects like, for example, the business sector or geopolitical factors. This makes it impossible to aggregate and quantify a general impact of the mentioned risks applicable to every infrastructure investment during their stages. However, clarifying the time-variant interdependence between the asset´s lifecycle phases and the underlying risk sources mentioned by the literature, helps potential investors to thoroughly evaluate the risk distribution of a potential infrastructure asset in the course of an adequate due diligence process. It can be concluded that investors should be aware of the severe differences in the magnitude and scope of the major risk sources emerging during the different lifecycle phases, assess them on an aggregated stage level and mitigate those risk types using suitable hedging, insurance and contractual measures.[63]

The potential to assess a performance pattern of direct infrastructure assets subject to these vast stream of risk sources is currently limited due to the lack of sufficient market data, but remains extremely important for evaluating the expected role of such assets within an institutional portfolio. In order to overcome this obstacle, recent academic literature, however, focuses on empirically identifying the historical risk-return profile of direct infrastructure investments which makes it possible to draw several conclusions about the general performance pattern that most direct infrastructure assets are likely to incorporate.

Thereby, the analyzed performance series in academic research are mainly derived from investments made by unlisted infrastructure funds and thus typically comprise appraisal-based data series focusing on rather mature infrastructure markets like in Australia, Canada or the United Kingdom. Table 4 gives a comprehensive overview of the most relevant empirical findings so far, which is limited to academic research, since the objectivity of insights available from several major infrastructure funds and investment banks cannot be guaranteed. In case that there is no annualized data given, the respective values for return and volatility are annualized by using standard calculus. Furthermore, it is worth noting that so far, only six academic studies investigated the performance of direct infrastructure assets in a thoroughly manner, meaning that the conclusions drawn by these results are still limited, but suitable to reveal some of the asset´s common risk-return features.

The empirical results show that direct infrastructure assets are generally outperformed by their listed counterparts in terms of annualized returns, but this superiority is also accompanied by a higher risk exposure in terms of volatility. However, compared to the other major investment classes, direct infrastructure assets demonstrate a historically superior risk-return profile. With regard to the claim whether they show equity-like returns with bond-like risks, it seems that the

[63] See, for example, Schaufelberger/Wipadapisut (2003), p. 212, for financial mitigation strategies.

risk-return profile of its asset class shows rather some similarity to direct property investments than to equity or bond investments in terms of the provided return and volatility data.

Considering the time period of the global financial crisis (2007-2009), Newell, Peng and De Francesco (2011) disclose a strongly protective character of direct infrastructure assets during the general market downturn. While the returns of listed assets like infrastructure stocks and general equities become negative and more volatile compared to their pre-crisis level, the asset class of direct infrastructure assets, in contrast, shows a sharp decline in its return, but it still remains positive and is accompanied by only a small raise in volatility (6.3 % up to 6.7 % versus 13.9 % up to 21.5 % for equities in general). A possible explanation for this behavior besides the relatively stable business model for infrastructure services seems to be the underlying valuation process. Since there is no standardized market for trading equity stakes of unlisted infrastructure assets, this type of asset, similar to direct property assets, is typically valued on an appraisal-base, so that general economic downturns, especially in the short-term, have not the same effect on the asset´s value as for listed investments which are valued in a more frequent manner.[64]

Two empirical studies analyze the cash flow behavior of unlisted direct infrastructure investments so far. Bitsch (2012) shows by analyzing the data of listed funds which are primarily investing in direct infrastructure assets that these assets generally provide less volatile, hence more stable cash flows than non-infrastructure assets. In terms of growth rate and volatility, the results indicate values of 6 % and 7 %, respectively, for the time period 2000-2010.[65] Bahceci and Weisdorf (2014) come to a similar conclusion, highlighting that infrastructure assets in general (unlisted and listed equity) have the lowest cash flow volatility and show a relatively low correlation with the other assets in their sample. With regard to the growth rates of the cash flows underlying their analysis, infrastructure investments rank between property assets and listed equities (S&P 500) in the sample.[66]

64 See Newell/Peng/De Francesco (2011), p. 72 or Humphreys/Maclean/Rogers (2016), p. 8.

65 See Bitsch (2012), p. 210.

66 See Bahceci/Weisdorf (2014), p. 34.

Table 4: Comparison of returns and volatilities (p.a.) of major asset classes in percent

Study	Period	Unlisted direct infrastructure	Listed infrastructure	Equities	Bonds	Unlisted direct property
Peng/Newell (2007)	1995-2006	14.1 / 5.8	22.4 / 16.0	12.9 / 11.0	7.2 / 4.3	10.9 / 1.5
Newell/Peng/ De Francesco (2011)	1995-2009	14.1 / 6.3	16.7 / 24.6	9.1 / 13.9	7.0 / 4.6	10.6 / 3.0
	2007-2009	8.2 / 6.7	-23.9 / 23.0	-13.2 / 21.5	7.1 / 6.9	3.3 / 5.8
Finkenzeller/ Dechant/Schäfers (2010)	1994-2009	8.0 / 3.8	14.8 / 16.6	7.7 / 15.0	8.1 / 4.9	9.4 / 4.9
Hartigan/Prasad/ De Francesco (2011)	1998-2008	12.7 / 6.5	13.8 / 13.6			12.5 / 3.2
Bird/Liem/Thorp (2014)	1995-2009	12.1 / 6.1	16.2 / 15.2			
Oyedele/Adair/ McGreal (2014)	2001-2010		6.0 / 14.3	4.7 / 19.0	3.5 / 3.8	
	2007-2009		-3.5 / 21.2	-19.2 / 32.6	-4.8/ 5.7	

Source: Own table, values correspond to annualized return/volatility in percent. Table based on Peng/Newell (2007), p. 438; Newell/Peng/De Francesco (2011), p. 66, p. 71; Finkenzeller/Dechant/Schäfers (2010), p. 265; Hartigan/Prasad/De Francesco (2011), p. 39; Bird/Liem/Thorp (2014), p. 808; Oyedele/Adair/McGreal (2014), p.8, p. 10.

Altogether, the empirical findings point out that direct infrastructure assets seem to rely on business models exhibiting relatively low risk levels while providing relatively high returns and stable cash flows. This tendency can also be supported when considering the interdependence between an asset´s expected return and systematic risk as provided by the capital asset pricing model (CAPM). Thereby, the asset beta as the unleveraged equity beta can be interpreted as a measure for the systematic operating risk of a company and thus should be similar for all companies with the same underlying business model irrespective of its status as listed or not. Taking a look at the asset beta´s value of listed infrastructure companies as an approximation for unlisted infrastructure assets, Rothballer and Kaserer (2012) find that the average infrastructure asset beta is 0.37 and thus considerably lower than the average value for non-infrastructure assets of 0.69.[67] Therefore, it can be concluded that infrastructure assets and their

[67] See Rothballer/Kaserer (2012), p. 99.

underlying business models are in terms of their systematic risk on average generally significantly less risky than non-infrastructure assets.

Analyzing the diversification potential of infrastructure assets, there are several studies indicating a relatively low correlation of direct infrastructure assets´ returns with those of other asset classes (see Table 5). The consistently highest correlation coefficients can be found with listed infrastructure investments (0.22 to 0.37). This tie is not surprising, since both types of assets rely on similar infrastructure business models which are subject to the same risk factors (see Table 3) that exert the same impact on the assets´ performance regardless of their status as listed or unlisted. Another relatively tight connection exists between direct infrastructure assets and unlisted direct property investments (0.20 to 0.51). Although some physical characteristics as well as risk factors are common to both assets, for instance, the indivisibility, a usually long-term investment horizon or the capital-intensive commitment, there are also certain differences between them, for example, the current market standardization, the feasibility of exit options or regulatory requirements.[68] In conjunction with the empirical results provided by Table 4 regarding the assets´ risk-return behavior, the current separation of property and infrastructure assets under the standard formula of Solvency II can be clearly underpinned.

Table 5: Correlation coefficients of direct infrastructure assets with other asset classes

Study	Period	Listed infrastructure	Equities	Bonds	Unlisted direct property
Peng/Newell (2007)	1995-2006	0.31	0.06	0.17	0.26
Newell/Peng/De Francesco (2011)	1995-2009	0.37	0.15	0.06	0.30
Finkenzeller/Dechant/Schäfers (2010)	1994-2009	0.29	0.27	-0.02	0.20
Hartigan/Prasad/De Francesco (2011)	1998-2008	0.22			0.51

Source: Own table, based on Peng/Newell (2007), p. 445; Newell/Peng/De Francesco (2011), p. 66; Finkenzeller/Dechant/Schäfers (2010), p. 267; Hartigan/Prasad/De Francesco (2011), p. 39.

In summary, based on the empirical findings, it can be confirmed that direct infrastructure assets have at least historically performed relatively well compared to other major asset classes. In general, they tend to provide stable and long-term cash flows, while they are also able to realize relatively high returns in combination with low volatilities and low correlation coefficients with other asset classes. In addition, the business models of infrastructure assets in general exhibit a relatively low level of systematic operating market risk as well as low marginal default rates. Furthermore, resulting from their long-term commitment, the generated cash flows offer the opportunity for narrowing the typical duration gap of insurance companies´ balance sheets,

68 See Finkenzeller/Dechant/Schäfers (2010), p. 266.

which is generally preferred by the design of Solvency II. However, there are severe caveats considering the risk profiles of such assets. Due to the lack of data, the impact of the vast variety of risk sources cannot be generalized to hold for every kind of infrastructure asset in the same manner. The allocation of the several risk types found in the literature to the typical lifecycle stages of such assets shows that there is a time-variant risk profile which finally causes a different risk exposure for an investor according to the current point in time of the assets´ lifespan. The total riskiness of a direct infrastructure asset, therefore, must be properly assessed by insurance companies for each infrastructure asset among every lifecycle stage. Altogether, it can be confirmed that direct infrastructure assets tend to show several properties that are unique for this sub asset-class and that according to these characteristics, they seem to be an appropriate investment opportunity for long-term investors like insurance companies, especially in the context of the prevailing low interest rate period. Thus, the following chapter 3, and in particular the section 3.2, will shed some light on the question whether and to what extent the regulatory treatment under Solvency II reflects these special characteristics in a prudentially manner. For a thorough comprehension and assessment of the complex requirements currently imposed by Solvency II, the subsequent section provides the theoretical foundation of the European insurance industry´s regulation regime and its main properties.

3 Regulatory treatment of direct infrastructure assets

The consideration that decisions of the asset-liability-management of an insurance company cannot be made purely based on economic deliberations, but are also subject to tax, accounting and especially regulatory constraints, offers the potential for a wide spread of different and complex investment combinations within the company's portfolio. In this sense, it is important to bear in mind that the European Union's insurance industry is still the largest institutional investor in the EU. In 2014, the total gross premiums of EU insurance companies reached € 1 169 billion and almost € 9 900 billion, which equals almost 63 % of the EU GDP, were globally invested in a wide range of assets.[69]

The past 2007-2009 financial crisis has impressively shown by using the example of the banking industry that weakly developed regulatory requirements can tremendously intensify an evolving economic turmoil. In times of highly interdependent cash flows, this turmoil can even emerge in a systemic risk which can lead through spillover effects to negative externalities for entire economies. However, not only the banking industry plays an important role for economic stability, but also the insurance industry with their unique characteristics. In this regard, Berger et al. (1997) highlight the insurance companies' role as financial intermediaries, investing the policyholders' premiums and providing economically important services like risk pooling and bearing as well as loss settlement services.[70] Especially, their role as financial intermediaries gains in importance against the growing academic background that assigns the role of a significant source of systemic risk to the insurance industry.[71]

In relation to the outcomes of that crisis, it is apparent that the enormous capital amounts of the EU insurance industry need to be regulated in a proper and risk-based way in order to incentivize risk oriented investment behavior and to fertilize the insurance industry's contribution to the sustainable development of the European Economic Area (EEA). Thus, the following section highlights the evolvement and the design of the recently introduced regulation regime Solvency II for the insurance industry in the EU.

3.1 Solvency II and its solvency capital requirement at a glance

The European insurance supervision regime has undergone substantial modifications by introducing the new regulation framework Solvency II (Directive 2009/138/EC), which finally came into effect in January 2016. The framework's introduction proceeded as a Lamfalussy process and was extended over a decade due to a continuous technical adjustment process induced by several quantitative impact studies. Thereby, the Directive 2009/138/EC was finally amended by the Omnibus II Directive (Directive 2014/51/EU) in 2014, which covers the technical treatment of several long-term guarantee issues.[72] In 2015, the Delegated Regulation (EU) 2015/35 comprising the implementing rules for Solvency II came into effect and was recently followed by a further amendment represented by the Delegated Regulation (EU)

[69] See Insurance Europe (2015a), p. 11 and p. 24.

[70] See Berger et al. (1997), p. 525.

[71] See, for example, Berdin and Sottocornola (2015).

[72] See McHugh and Schiffel, 2014, p. 1.

2016/467 in 2016, which covers the current changes in the calculation of the capital requirements for several asset classes typically held by insurance companies like, for instance, infrastructure assets.

The traceable necessity of the new regulation regime emerged from several severe shortcomings of the prior regulation framework Solvency I, for example, the non-risk sensitive and one-model-fits-all determination of capital requirements or the exploitation of regulatory arbitrage due to low levels of regulatory harmonization within the European Union.[73] When assessing the total risk exposure of an insurance company aroused by its asset-liability interaction, Solvency I did not sufficiently take some major important risk sources into account, for instance, market, credit or operational risks and thus, led to a distorted picture of the company's true solvency situation.[74] In order to overcome these deficiencies, Solvency II has been introduced by considering several main aims, for instance amongst others, to implement a risk-oriented capital determination for the investment purposes of insurance companies, to harmonize the EU-wide insurance regulation regime and thus to avoid any regulatory arbitrage, as well as to strengthen the policyholders' protection level and to enforce a competitive market structure for the whole European insurance industry.[75]

In practice, the Solvency II framework consists of three fundamental pillars. The first pillar is related to a risk-oriented determination of two capital ratios, the solvency capital requirement (SCR) and a lower capital threshold, the minimum capital requirement (MCR), by either using a generally applicable standard formula or an internal model which needs to be previously approved by a supervisory authority. The violation of one of these two capital requirements can cause different supervisory interventions depending on the scope of deviating from these thresholds, even including a withdrawal of the business license as the ultima ratio in case of breaching the MCR. Furthermore, the first pillar deploys the basic rules for market consistent valuation purposes and the identification of the insurance company's own funds to cover these capital requirements. The second pillar refers to requirements for the insurance company's risk management and governance system, for instance, by obliging insurance companies to carry out the Own Risk and Solvency Assessment (ORSA) in order to detect any risk deviations from those used for the regulatory capital determination. In addition, it sets out further details of the supervisory review process. The third pillar is dedicated to requirements for enhancing the reporting quality, transparency, market discipline and public disclosure.[76]

Both capital requirements are calculated in a forward-looking manner based on an insurance company's economic balance sheet, which implies a market oriented valuation of assets and liabilities as a cornerstone. The market value of assets can either be derived from capital markets (mark-to-market approach), if there is an active and liquid market for the asset or otherwise by means of standard financial models (mark-to-model approach). Regarding the insurance company's liabilities, for which usually no market exists in order to derive prices, their valuation is based on a best estimate in conjunction with an obligatory risk margin. The

[73] See van Hulle (2011), p. 179.

[74] See European Commission (2015), question 2.

[75] See van Hulle (2011), pp. 179-180.

[76] See van Hulle (2011), pp. 180-181; European Commission (2015), question 2.

resulting amount is balanced as the company's technical provisions and is intended to disclose the current price of an immediate transfer of the whole insurance portfolio to a third party.[77]

From a technical point of view, the SCR is calibrated as the Value at Risk (VaR) of the insurance company's basic own funds at a confidence level of 99.5 % over a one-year period. It is intended to cover all quantifiable risks for the existing business as well as for the expected new business during the following year.[78] In other words, this ratio technically ensures that the probability of an exceedance of a potential loss over the insurance company's equity stake under normal circumstances on any given year is 0.5 %. This is equivalent to the interpretation that the VaR measure corresponds to the expectation of an insurance company's insolvency only once in a 200 year's period of time. Even though this measure relates to a high level of technical solvency, in practice, the actual probability of insolvency tends to be even much lower, since the SCR is embedded with extensive supervisory intervention techniques. Insurance companies are also obliged to continuously qualitatively and quantitatively assess any deviation from their latest reported risk profiles in order to assess whether the SCR significantly over- or underestimates the underlying risk profile.[79] Depending on the corresponding outcome, the insurance company can either alter its risk profile be restructuring its asset portfolio or in case of severe deviations, it can be forced by the supervision authority to recalculate its SCR and to raise further equity capital.[80]

The SCR according to the standard formula is determined based on a modular approach consisting of six main risk modules, namely, market risk module, non-life risk module, health risk module, default risk module, life risk module and the intangible risk module. Except for the default and intangible risk modules, each of these modules is further subdivided into different risk sub-modules, covering the explicitly technical treatment of the capital determination for the underlying risk sources (see Figure 1).

[77] See Bauer/Reuss/Singer (2012) p. 455.

[78] See EIOPA (2014a), pp. 6-7.

[79] See BaFin (2015), paragraph 8; Directive 2009/138/EG, article 102.

[80] See BaFin (2015), paragraphs 12 and 13.

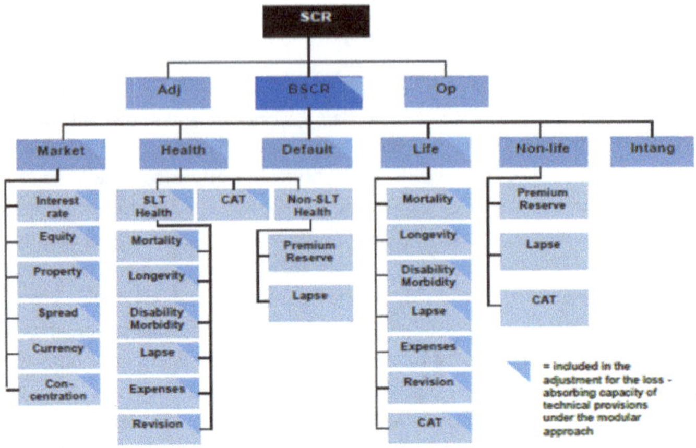

Figure 1: Modular approach of the SCR-determination (Source: EIOPA (2014a), p. 6).

For each of these risk sources, a SCR is determined by predefined calculation approaches either using a factor or scenario model. Considering the factor model, for some risks like, for instance, the premium and reserve risk, the capital requirement is calculated by applying given risk factors to a corresponding balance sheet value at the statement date. Whereas for other risks that need to be assessed by scenario models, the given risk factors are applied as instantaneous economic stress scenarios on the corresponding balance sheet values in order to take the entire balance sheet's dynamics into account. Thus, determining the capital requirement is consistent with the risk source's net impact on the level of the basic own funds, which is measured as the change in the difference between the market values of the assets and liabilities before and after the economic stress (see Figure 2).

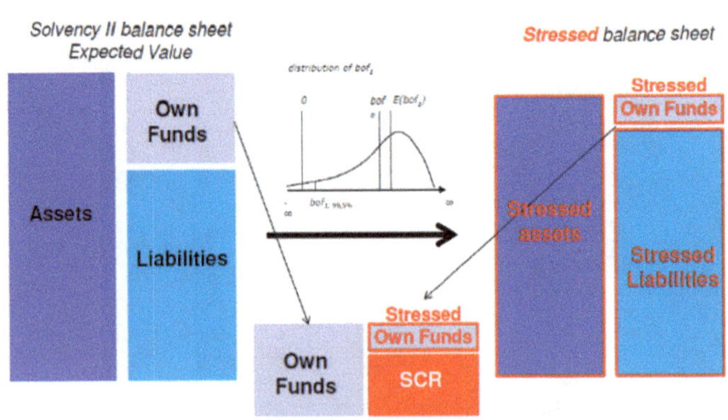

Figure 2: SCR as residual net equity stake from the stressed balance sheet (Source: EIOPA (2014a), p. 7).

In order to obtain the insurance company's overall SCR, the capital requirements of the individual sub-modules are subject to two mitigation channels, namely diversification effects between the individual risk sources and the loss absorbing effects of the technical provisions.[81] The latter channel relates to capital reliefs, for instance, by a lower future surplus participation for policyholders or by a decline in the tax liability. The diversification effects emerge in a capital reduction through the aggregation of the individual solvency capital requirements for the sub-modules to capital requirements for each main risk module, which in turn, are combined to an overall basic solvency capital requirement (BSCR) illustrated by equation (1).[82] According to the latest QIS 5 impact study, both mitigation channels are important capital reliefs for insurance companies, with average proportions of the total SCR of 32 % for diversification effects and 57 % for adjustment effects.[83]

$$\mathrm{BSCR}=\sqrt{\sum_{i,j}\mathrm{Corr}_{i,j}\cdot\mathrm{SCR}_i\cdot\mathrm{SCR}_j}+\mathrm{SCR}_{\mathrm{intangibles}} \qquad (1)$$

where $\mathrm{Corr}_{i,j}$ denotes the correlation matrix containing the correlation coefficients between the individual, modular based solvency capital requirements $\mathrm{SCR}_{i,j}$ and $\mathrm{SCR}_{\mathrm{intangibles}}$ stands for the solvency capital requirement for the intangible asset risk module.

Even if the modular approach of the standard formula covers a vast scope of different risk sources, not all quantifiable risks relevant for some insurance companies are explicitly covered, for instance, inflation risk, reputation risk, liquidity risk, contagion risk or legal environment risk are missing risk sources.[84] Since insurance companies are obliged to identify any deviation of their risk profiles in comparison to those used in the SCR determination by the Own Risk and Solvency Assessment (ORSA), these risk sources are, however, still implicitly covered, too.

3.2 Direct infrastructure assets under Solvency II

As chapter 2 highlights, direct infrastructure assets with their unique characteristics regarding their risk-return profiles and their past performance are increasingly focused by the investment purposes of insurance companies. But their regulatory capital requirements under Solvency II are of particular importance for an insurance company´s decision to take any infrastructure exposure into its portfolio, because the over- or underestimation of the assets´ risk contribution to the company´s portfolio can cause an extreme regulatory capital burden.[85]

Against the current background of tight public budgets and in order to incentivize capital markets for financing infrastructure assets, there has been a fierce debate about the right regulatory treatment of such assets among politicians, scientists, supervisors and investors. Its current treatment, consequently, has undergone significant changes through the recent implementation of the amendments represented by the Delegated Regulation (EU) 2016/467, which came into force in April 2016. The cornerstone of the new regulation is the explicit

[81] See EIOPA (2014b), p. 127.

[82] See Delegated Regulation (EU) 2015/35, section 3, subsection 5 (87).

[83] See EIOPA (2011), p. 63.

[84] See EIOPA (2014a), p. 9.

[85] See Gatzert/Kosub (2014) for a comprehensive overview of the regulatory treatment of infrastructure investments other than direct infrastructure assets.

consideration of an own and tailored asset class for qualifying equity and debt investments in the field of infrastructure. For the case of qualifying equity investments, this asset class is currently explicitly limited to certain infrastructure projects using a special purpose vehicle (SPV).[86] Due to this restriction towards a special form of legal framework, the new asset class only represents a specific subset of the entire legal range of infrastructure equity investments, thus, inducing EIOPA to suggest an additional enhancement of the infrastructure asset class in June 2016 in order to capture also equity investments in infrastructure corporates as another legal form.[87] It is commonly expected that the European Commission follows this advice made by EIOPA and will make some further amendments to the Delegated Regulation (EU) 2015/35.

In order to evaluate the appropriateness of the current regulatory treatment of direct infrastructure assets under Solvency II, it is important to reconsider their usually underlying legal form at first. From the perspective of the insurance company as the potential investor, these investments are commonly treated as private investments in unlisted equity.[88] Thereby, investors need to acquire or build up a sufficient equity stake of the underlying infrastructure asset in order to receive ownership rights and control over the asset´s generated cash flows. From a legal perspective, and independently from the underlying infrastructure asset, such an infrastructure investment is commonly structured as either a project entity, represented by special purpose vehicles (SPVs) or limited purpose entities (LPEs), or as a corporate entity.[89] In this context, an infrastructure SPV typically represents an entity that is only established for special purposes related to the treatment of one single infrastructure asset within a limited period of time, for example, to construct or operate a single power plant.[90] Whereas an infrastructure corporate acts as an entity without a limited lifetime and is usually permitted to simultaneously own and operate multiple infrastructure assets.[91]

The main rationale behind these legal structures, however, is to protect the insurance company´s remaining assets from financial risks stemming from the variety of risks underlying the infrastructure asset. Since these can be tremendous in their magnitude as pointed out in chapter 2.2, these legal structuring procedures ensure a financially strong safety level and constitute only a limited liability for the investor. Consequently, it is reasonable, and already partly implemented under Solvency II through the recent enforcement of the Delegated Regulation (EU) 2016/467, to refine the equity risk sub-module within the standard formula´s market risk module in order to align the regulatory treatment of an infrastructure equity investment to its usual legal structure in practice. Thereby, the new regulatory specifications are able to incorporate the existing risk differences stemming from different legal structures, for instance, differences in the total level of exposure to infrastructure risk sources if the investment made

[86] See EIOPA (2016a), p. 5.

[87] See EIOPA (2016a), published in June 2016.

[88] See EIOPA (2016a), p. 8.

[89] See Insurance Europe (2015b), answer, p. 2.

[90] See Insurance Europe (2015b), answer, p. 2; EIOPA (2016b), p. 1.

[91] See EIOPA (2016b), p. 1.

by the insurance company comprises only a single or multiple infrastructure assets (SPV versus corporate structure).

Besides the existing treatment of equity investments in general, the current design of the Solvency II standard formula, therefore, is intended to incorporate and to differentiate infrastructure equity investments according to their status whether and where they are listed (listed versus unlisted equities) as well as whether they comply with several qualifying criteria inducing a lower risk profile on average and thus, advocate in favor of a lower regulatory capital charge (Table 6).

Table 6: Current capital charges for infrastructure equity investments under Solvency II

	non-qualifying equity	qualifying equity	
		infrastructure project	infrastructure corporate (final advice)
listed equity (EEA/OECD)	Type 1: 39 % + symmetric adjustment	30 % + 77 % symmetric adjustment	30 % + 77 % symmetric adjustment (project like) or 36 % + symmetric adjustment
unlisted equity (EEA/OECD)	Type 2: 49 % + symmetric adjustment	30 % + 77 % symmetric adjustment	30 % + 77 % symmetric adjustment (project like) or 36 % + symmetric adjustment

Source: Own table, based on EIOPA (2016a), p 5; Delegated Regulation (EU) 2016/467, article 1 (4, section 6); Delegated Regulation (EU) 2015/35, article 168 (1-3).

Regarding the principle view of Solvency II, equity investments are basically not considered to be sensitive to changes in the interest rate term structure and thus have to be considered in the equity risk sub-module according to the technical specifications provided by EIOPA (2014b), paragraph SCR 5.18.[92] Thereby, the Directive 2009/138/EC, article 105 (5), and the Delegated Regulation (EU) 2015/35, article 168 (1-3), distinguish between type 1 and type 2 equities. Whereas type 1 equities incorporate equities listed in regulated markets in the EEA or OECD, type 2 equities cover equities perceived to be generally more risky, like those not listed in the EEA or OECD, non-listed and private equities, commodities and other alternative investments.[93]

A direct infrastructure asset, if it is not of a strategic nature, is basically assigned to the classification of type 2 equities. Therefore, its regulatory capital requirement needs to cover the loss in the basic own funds that results from an instantaneous decline in its market value through

[92] See EIOPA (2014b), p. 141.

[93] See Delegated Regulation (EU) 2015/35, article 168 (1-3).

the application of a predetermined shock factor of 49 %.[94] In addition, the symmetric adjustment mechanism has to be applied in order to mitigate effects from the market´s pro-cyclical investment behavior. Its value is continuously provided by EIOPA and enables the applicable shock factor to move within a range of 39 % to 59 % (± 10 %). In order to capture diversification benefits between the certain types of equity investments, unlisted infrastructure equity is assumed to be correlated by a coefficient of 0.75 with type 1 equities and to be perfectly positive correlated to all equities considered to be type 2.[95]

Referring to the usual legal structures of infrastructure equity investments, the amended specifications introduce a new separate asset class for qualifying infrastructure equity investments within the equity risk sub-module. In case that the investment is not of a strategic nature, the required capital charge for this type of equity investment is substantially lowered to 30 % in addition to 77 % of the symmetric adjustment´s value.[96] This capital charge is applicable independently from the fact whether the equity investment is listed or not, as long as it can be classified as a qualifying equity investment. In order to fall into this classification, the infrastructure investment needs to fulfill several specific criteria which are summarized as follows.[97] The underlying infrastructure entity has to be structured as a project entity in terms of a SPV that is only permitted to develop, finance, operate and own a single underlying infrastructure asset. Further, it needs to meet its financial obligations even under sustained stress scenarios, given the cash flows are predictable and exhibit a certain stability in their occurrence, for example, through purchase agreements with particular parties like governments. The infrastructure project entity needs to be equipped with a contractual framework in order to ensure a high degree of financial protection through revenue loss arrangements as well as to provide a sufficient amount of reserve funds. Furthermore, in case that there is no external credit rating for the infrastructure entity available, it has to be located in the EEA or OECD. In addition, there are further specifying requirements considering the entity´s risk management and due diligence, aiming on mitigation of some typical risk sources, for example, construction risk, operating or refinancing risk. The supervision regime considers the compliance of direct infrastructure assets with these requirements as a risk mitigation technique that induces, on average, a better risk profile compared to other infrastructure assets, thus justifying a lower regulatory capital charge.

This type of infrastructure equity investment is also assumed to show diversification effects with other types of equity investments and it is thus correlated by a coefficient of 0.75 with type 1 equities and perfectly positive correlated with all equities considered to be type 2.[98] Therefore, the calculation of the solvency capital requirement of the equity risk sub-module is adjusted as follows:[99]

---

[94] See Delegated Regulation (EU) 2015/35, article 169 (2).

[95] See Delegated Regulation (EU) 2015/35, article 168 (4).

[96] See Delegated Regulation (EU) 2016/467, article 1 (4, section 6).

[97] See Delegated Regulation (EU) 2016/467, article 1 (4, section 1-2) for the criteria.

[98] See Delegated Regulation (EU) 2016/467, article 1 (4, section 5).

[99] See Delegated Regulation (EU) 2016/467, article 1 (4, section 5).

$$SCR_{equity}=\sqrt{SCR_{type\ 1\ equities}^2+2\cdot 0.75\cdot SCR_{type\ 1\ equities}\cdot(SCR_{type\ 2\ equities}+SCR_{qinf})+(SCR_{type\ 2\ equities}+SCR_{qinf})^2}\quad(2)$$

where: $SCR_{type\ 1\ equities}$ denotes the capital requirement for type 1 equities, $SCR_{type\ 2\ equities}$ stands for the capital requirement for type 2 equities and SCR_{qinf} comprises the capital requirement for qualifying infrastructure equities.

In June 2016, EIOPA published its final technical advice concerning the regulatory treatment of infrastructure corporates. The cornerstone of the new advice is the proposal of introducing a further infrastructure asset class only reserved for qualifying equity investments in infrastructure corporates. In principle, it stipulates a 36 % capital charge in combination with the usual symmetric adjustment mechanism for both, listed and unlisted qualifying corporate equity investments.[100] In addition, it is intended that specific infrastructure corporates which exhibit an equivalent level of risk compared to infrastructure SPVs, are permitted to be similarly treated, i.e. with a capital charge of 30 % plus the adjusted symmetric adjustment.[101] The superior criterion to fall into the category of equity investments in qualifying infrastructure corporates, and in contrast to project-like investments, is that the majority of the corporate's revenue need to be derived from six specific infrastructure sectors within the geographic area of the EEA or OECD. The permitted business sectors include the generation, transmission or distribution of electrical or thermal energy, distribution or transmission of natural or petroleum gas, provision of water or wastewater services, waste management or recycling services, transport networks or the operation of transport assets and finally social infrastructure.[102] Furthermore, there are similar requirements to those established for the qualification of infrastructure projects, for example, the demand of a high level of predictability and stability of the underlying cash flows, a protective contractual framework for the investors as well as similar parts of the investment's risk management and due diligence processes. The infrastructure corporate must also provide a credit quality step of at least 3 or in case that such a rating does not exist, it needs to exhibit at least 3 years of operational business experience.[103] EIOPA suggests for diversification effects a correlation coefficient of 0.75 with type 1 equities and a perfectly positive correlation with all equities considered to be type 2.[104]

According to the industry's comments accompanying both final reports published by EIOPA, there has been much concern within the insurance industry about the appropriateness of the new form of regulatory treatment of infrastructure equity investments.[105] There are various arguments for a contrary viewpoint to EIOPA's opinion that are not only driven by the interest of the insurance industry. Considering the widely discussed entire bunch of qualifying criteria, it is currently not possible to assess their appropriateness in practice, since the market for infrastructure equity assets is still immature and their performances under solvency

---

[100] See EIOPA (2016a), p 5.

[101] See EIOPA (2016a), p 5.

[102] See EIOPA (2016a), p 20.

[103] See EIOPA (2016a), p 20.

[104] See EIOPA (2016a), p 7.

[105] See EIOPA (2015a), pp. 13-15; EIOPA (2016a), pp. 7-9.

requirements have not been scientifically investigated yet. But the fact that those criteria are derived from a specific portfolio of listed infrastructure assets raises justified concern about their general fitting to the usual properties of direct infrastructure assets that are unlisted and according to the results of chapter 2, tend to be less risky than their listed counterparts. This actually requires a further lowering of the capital charge, since the current threshold of 30 % is derived from the properties of listed assets and hence leads to a discrepancy that might induce a discrimination of investors in terms of the regulatory capital burden when they are investing in unlisted assets.

In this context, EIOPA itself explicitly states that empirical data suggest a capital charge below 20 %, but it argues to set a lower bound of 30 % due to the limitation of the representativeness of the empirical data.[106] Notwithstanding the lack of data, the approximation of the capital charge by the behavior of listed assets neglects the influence of general market movements on the assets′ market values, which seems to be immanent in practice. Frequently quoted market prices for listed equities and the less frequently determined appraisal-valuations for unlisted equities are usually subject to different valuation points in time and hence underlie a different impact of general market movements on their values.[107] This fact can also be seen when considering the empirical results provided by Newell, Peng and De Francesco (2011) and Oyedele, Adair and McGreal (2014), given in Table 4, showing that during the highly volatile global financial crisis (2007-2009), the returns of direct infrastructure assets behaved still less volatile than those of their listed counterparts and remained even positive (8.2/6.7 versus 23.9/23.0 in terms of annualized return/volatility).

However, EIOPA considers both types of infrastructure assets, listed and unlisted, to be subject to the same risk contribution only stemming from its infrastructure business model, independently from its status as listed or not, and hence neglects the influence of any market movements on the assets′ values.[108] This, on the one hand, can be definitely underpinned when taking the same systematic operating risk factor for both types of assets into account (asset beta, see chapter 2.2). On the other hand, the empirically inferred results of a better and less volatile return behavior of unlisted infrastructure assets during the financial crisis, however, can only be explained by the existence of a stronger influence of market movements on the return behavior of the listed assets, caused by differences in the market and appraisal-based valuations.[109] It can be concluded that this difference in the commonly used valuation techniques, and thereby the difference in the assets` exposures to market movements, should be considered by EIOPA more strongly when assessing the capital charge for infrastructure assets.

Furthermore, if the direct infrastructure asset is not able to comply with the qualifying criteria, investors are only permitted to classify it as a type 2 asset, thus stipulating a regulatory capital charge similar to investments in hedge funds for instance, that seems to be definitely not justified in accordance with the asset′s historic performance pattern and its general properties

[106] See EIOPA (2015a), p 14.

[107] See Newell/Peng/De Francesco (2011), p. 72; AustralianSuper (2013), p.4.

[108] See EIOPA (2016a), p 54.

[109] For example, AustralianSuper (2013), p.4; Newell/Peng/De Francesco (2011), p. 72 or Humphreys/Maclean/Rogers (2016), p. 8.

(both see chapter 2). Thus, it might be the case that the qualifying criteria act as an additional constraint for the future emergence of the infrastructure market in Europe, which contradicts the European Commission´s aim of fostering capital markets for financing infrastructure assets, and thus impedes the possibility in future to collect data of the performance of direct infrastructure assets within insurance companies` portfolios.

The second widely discussed area of criticism considers the adequate level of the correlation coefficients applicable to direct infrastructure assets under the standard formula. A different viewpoint to EIOPA´s opinion can be underpinned by the empirical results of the risk-return profiles mentioned in chapter 2.2. The comparison of the coefficients determined by EIOPA with those provided by Table 5, indicating a range between 0.06 and 0.27 for direct (unlisted) infrastructure with equities in general, shows that the implemented coefficients of Solvency II tend to be higher as actually indicated according to the empirical results (see chapter 2.2, Bitsch (2012), Bahceci and Weisdorf (2014) and Rothballer and Kaserer (2012)). Hence, it limits the investor´s potential to benefit from diversification effects within the solvency capital requirements. In particular, coefficients that are implemented at a higher level than empirically justified, might rather work as an additional solvency capital charge and thus implicitly raising the corresponding module´s safety level. Thereby, it is likely that this induces additional investment barriers for this type of asset, because insurance companies are obliged to bear a higher regulatory capital burden than actually necessary.

Therefore, the recently enforced lower capital charges for qualifying infrastructure equity investments in terms of SPVs and the intended lower charges for infrastructure corporates in comparison to a type 2 classification under Solvency II, are indeed justified, in particular when applying the required qualifying criteria. However, since the appropriateness of these criteria is questionable at least due to their determination approach, it seems to be justified under consideration of the empirical results so far, and when maintaining the differentiation between the different legal structures underlying direct infrastructure assets, to further lower the capital charges for both, SPVs and corporates, independently from a compliance with the qualifying criteria. The determination of an own regulatory capital charge for the infrastructure asset in chapter 4.4.2 yields a threshold of 15.1 %, which is sufficient to cover losses in the infrastructure asset´s market value in 99.5 % of cases. Thus, it can be clearly argued in favor of lowering the current risk charges for unlisted equity investments at least below the current threshold of 30 %, which the empirical data by EIOPA actually indicate, too. This request is also mainly in line with the general viewpoint of the insurance industry.[110] Furthermore, it seems to be also justified to clearly reduce the currently high correlation coefficients for both types of direct infrastructure assets.

A further critical point, and yet mainly neglected in the current debates of the regulatory treatment of direct infrastructure assets, refers to their exposure to shifts in the interest rate term structure. Due to their appraisal-based valuation in practice, which is mainly based on discounting techniques, their market values are strongly depending on the current and expected level of the risk-free interest rate. Furthermore, since infrastructure investments tend to generate long-term and stable cash flows, they indeed show a slight similarity to the usual characteristics

[110] See EIOPA (2015a), for example the comment made by GDV, pp. 45-46.

of fixed-income instruments, apart from the legal differences, for example, in the validity of claims and ownership rights on the underlying cash flows.[111] According to EIOPA´s guidelines, insurance companies should, in case of an asset with equity and debt instrument characteristics, consider both features and choose that corresponding risk sub-module, which is consistent with the predominant economic substance of the asset.[112] Even if equity investments in infrastructure are explicitly specified to be treated within the equity risk sub-module, the extent to which such an investment shows fixed-income characteristics and thus rather demands a treatment within the interest rate risk sub-module, should be considered in future academic research and political discussion in a more intense manner.[113] Referring to the infrastructure asset developed in chapter 4, a regulatory treatment within the interest rate sub-module, however, leads to a lower capital requirement than in the equity risk sub-module, but it provides a first insight into a possible discrepancy (see chapter 4.3.3).

[111] The hybrid characteristics of direct infrastructure assets between equity and fixed-income, is mentioned, amongst others, by Inderst (2010), p. 78 or Newell/Peng (2008), p. 25.

[112] See EIOPA (2015b), p. 3.

[113] A written request to GDV and Deutsche Aktuarvereinigung for clarification remained without reply.

4 Optimal capital allocation and solvency capital requirements for the insurance company

Infrastructure equity investments tend to be a profitable investment opportunity for large institutional investors like insurance companies, at least in a stylized manner (see chapter 2). However, as a result of the immaturity and heterogeneity of the infrastructure asset class and the prevailing lack of data, the overall performance of an insurance company's portfolio investing in infrastructure equity assets is yet not clear, as well as the asset's contribution to the overall riskiness of the portfolio and the resulting regulatory capital requirements to cover potential losses stemming from these risks. Furthermore, the question of an optimal asset composition of a portfolio investing in an illiquid asset like unlisted infrastructure equity still remains open under solvency requirements.

In order to clarify these open issues about direct infrastructure assets, a market oriented valuation model referring to the typical lifecycle phases of infrastructure assets as explained in chapter 2 is developed. The academic literature on modelling and evaluating infrastructure assets is scarce, but several different modelling and valuation approaches have been evolved over the last decade, for example, discounted cash flow models (DCF), option pricing models or nested simulation techniques, but none of them seems to generally provide any clear superiority in capturing the infrastructure asset's typical characteristics and performance. Thus, the following chapter aims to contribute to this research stream by developing and evaluating an own valuation model.

4.1 Valuation model of a direct infrastructure asset

Based on the existing literature on modelling infrastructure assets, the theoretical framework of discounted cash flow models, partially in combination with rules of thumb, is a commonly used valuation approach for infrastructure assets in research and practice.[114] This approach basically consists of two components, namely a projection of the asset's future cash flows and a risk-adjusted discount factor reflecting the return requirements for the possible investor. For the case of infrastructure assets, the lack of market data makes it difficult to calibrate both components in a market oriented manner. However, with regard to the findings in chapter 2 concerning the asset's risk-return profile, and in consideration of the general acceptance of DCF-models for valuation purposes within the Solvency II framework,[115] this kind of valuation model seems to be still appropriate, and even reliable, to reflect the unique characteristics of an infrastructure asset within a market oriented valuation approach.

4.1.1 Model framework

With respect to the first component of a DCF valuation, namely the projection of the asset's future cash flows, the infrastructure asset's total cash flow stream can be usually decomposed into individual sub-streams in order to reflect differences in the asset's typical lifecycle phases

---

[114] See, for example, Jeong et al. (2016), Espinoza/Morris (2013), Wibowo/Alfen (2013), Ho/Liu (2002).

[115] See EIOPA (2015c), guideline 3, pp. 3-4.

and its general transition from a greenfield asset into a maturing brownfield asset.[116] For the intended valuation model used in the following setting, the whole cash flow stream is divided into three main streams, namely one stream for the construction costs (C), one for the operating cash flows (CF^{OP}) and one for the decommissioning cash flows (CF^{D}). This division seems to be reasonable, because it reflects the asset's typical changes in the shape of its risk distribution along its lifespan in greater detail (see Table 3). Thereby, it is intended to approximate the distinctive differences in the scope of risks between the three phases by changing the individual growth factors of the asset's costs and cash flows as well as their volatility. By assuming that each amount of costs or cash flow occurs at the end of a year and that the asset's total lifespan is expected to be 20 years, the intended construction period lasts for 3 years, the operating phase for 12 years and the decommissioning phase for 5 years, which is consistent with common assumptions in the literature. After 20 years, it is assumed that the asset is completely worthless, since this can happen in practice as the worst case result of the infrastructure asset's inherent illiquidity risk, for instance, through an expired and non-renewed concession. Finally, it is assumed that the asset's cash flows are totally realizable for the insurance company as the exclusive equity investor. The time-variant occurrence of the corresponding construction costs and cash flows over the asset's lifetime is illustrated in Figure 3.

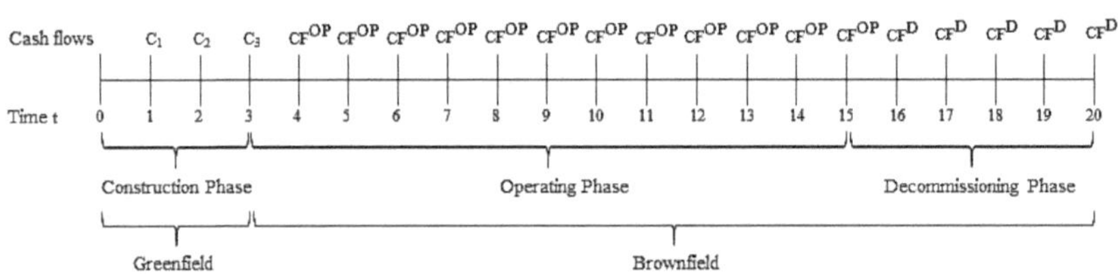

Figure 3: Time depending cash flow stream of the infrastructure asset (Source: Own figure).

Modeling construction costs

As shown by data from Moody's, the construction period of infrastructure assets exerts a significant and strong influence on the asset's overall performance (see chapter 2), leading to its consideration as a main and critical driving force behind the performance of the infrastructure asset in this setting.[117] Therefore, modeling and calibrating the period's stream of costs in a careful manner is of high relevance for the whole simulation results. Building on the approaches of Wibowo and Alfen (2013) and Ho and Liu (2002), the dynamics of the construction costs at time t are intended to follow a Geometric Brownian Motion (GBM), thus leading to log-normally distributed costs.[118] This stochastic process ensures that the stochastic costs are non-negative, which is also consistent with an economic interpretation of costs.

[116] The approach of decomposing the asset's total cash flow stream into individual sub-streams (mainly construction costs and operating cash flows) can be found, for example, in Jeong et al. (2016).

[117] See Moody's (2013), p. 18.

[118] See Wibowo/Alfen (2013), p .412 and Ho/Liu (2002), p. 147.

Therefore, the construction costs of the infrastructure asset follow the stochastic differential equation (SDE) under the real-world condition given by equation (3).[119]

$$dC(t)=\mu_C C(t)dt+\sigma_C C(t)dW_C(t) \tag{3}$$

where: $dC(t)$ denotes the incremental change in the construction costs within a short period of time dt, μ_C stands for the constant drift of the costs, $C(t)$ for the value of the construction costs at time t, σ_C for the constant volatility coefficient of the construction costs and $dW_C(t)$ denotes a standard Wiener process (Brownian Motion) for the construction costs. Thereby, the constant drift term can be interpreted as the general (long-term) movement of the costs and the second term consisting of the volatility coefficient and the standard Wiener process as the diffusion term that exerts a constant random noise to the general drift.

The SDE given in equation (3) has the analytic solution provided by equation (4) and in discretized form by equation (5), which is used for the implementation in a Monte Carlo simulation.[120]

$$C(t)=C(0)\cdot\exp((\mu_C-\frac{\sigma_C^2}{2})t+\sigma_C W_C(t)) \tag{4}$$

$$C(t)=C(t-1)\cdot\exp((\mu_C-\frac{\sigma_C^2}{2})\Delta t+\sigma_C\sqrt{\Delta t}Z(t)) \tag{5}$$

where: $C(t)$ denotes the value of the construction costs at time t, μ_C stands for the constant drift of the costs, σ_C for the constant diffusion or volatility coefficient of the construction costs, Δt for the discrete length of the time increment, $W_C(t)$ for the standard Wiener process (Brownian Motion) of the construction costs at time t and Z(t) denotes independent and identical standard-normally distributed variables at time t.

For the purpose of calibrating the process, the parameters given by Ho and Liu (2002) are used and slightly adjusted.[121] The constant drift μ_C in terms of an annualized constant cost growth rate is assumed to be 4 % and the constant volatility σ_C to be 10 % per annum. Despite the lack of sufficient market data, these values are still reasonable when considering the usually main drivers of construction costs, namely material prices and labor wages. The growth rate of both drivers, approximated by the annual inflation rate and the annual growth rate of labor costs, can be used for an economically boundary condition that the annual construction costs′ growth rate must at least exceed in this setting. Considering data provided by the OECD (2016b), the average annual inflation rate over the period 2010-2015 was 1.82 %, while its forecast for 2017 is 2.0 %. The average annual growth rate for the unit labor costs over the same period was 0.91 %.[122] Choosing a higher level for the construction costs′ growth factor compared to these economic boundary conditions seems to be justified, since the construction of infrastructure assets usually requires special knowledge in construction theory and expensive materials due to the intended long-term availability of their services.

---

119 In accordance with Albrecht/Maurer (2008), p. 177 for the general solution of the GBM.

120 In accordance with Albrecht/Maurer (2008), p. 175 and for the general solution of the GBM, p. 185.

121 See Ho/Liu (2002), p. 152.

122 See OECD (2016b), statistics about the inflation rate (CPI), inflation rate forecast and the unit labor costs.

The value of the construction costs′ volatility coefficient σ_C of 10 % is assumed to be lower than suggested by Ho and Liu (2002) which used a value of 20 %. One the one hand, a relatively high level for this parameter can generally be underpinned by the empirical findings of Flyvbjerg, Holm and Buhl (2003) for example, showing that the global cost escalation of transport infrastructure projects amounts on average to 28 %.[123] This high value for cost overruns illustrates that a projection of future infrastructure costs is usually relatively error-prone, thus justifying a high level for the diffusion coefficient in order to reflect possible cost escalations for simulation purposes. On the other hand, a lower value is finally chosen for the model′s calibration, because insurance companies can be assumed to have a profound knowledge on estimating risk factors and their resulting costs, and in addition, as investors in infrastructure equity, they are obliged to show some experience in the area of overseeing projects under construction when applying for the qualifying equity risk sub-module under Solvency II.[124]

The present literature does not provide many insights for the adequate choice of the starting value C(0) of the construction cost′s process. In most studies, the net present value is even negative and turned into a positive value by using a real option approach.[125] For the following setting, therefore, the starting value C(0) is assumed to be a multiple of the starting value of the operating cash flow stream by the factor 2.0, which, in conjunction with the high levels of the drift and diffusion terms, is believed to reflect a relatively high riskiness of the construction period for the overall performance of the asset.

Modeling operating cash flows

Due to the non-negativity condition of the GBM, this stochastic process is also suitable for modeling the infrastructure asset′s cash flows stemming from the operating phase. The empirical findings about infrastructure cash flows indicate that these are relatively stable, less volatile and weakly correlated with non-infrastructure cash flows (see chapter 2.2), and hence there is no indication for a mean reverting behavior. This is in contrast to the opinion of EIOPA, considering the evolution of stock prices and their returns to follow a mean-reverting behavior in general.[126] Therefore, the operating cash flows will follow the dynamics of a GBM given by equations (6) and (7).

$$dCF^{OP}(t)=\mu_{OP}CF^{OP}(t)dt+\sigma_{OP}CF^{OP}(t)dW_{OP}(t) \tag{6}$$

$$CF^{OP}(t)=CF^{OP}(t\text{-}1)\cdot\exp((\mu_{OP}\text{-}\frac{\sigma_{OP}^2}{2})\Delta t+\sigma_{OP}\sqrt{\Delta t}Z(t)) \tag{7}$$

where: $CF^{OP}(t)$ denotes the value of the operating cash flows at time t, μ_{OP} stands for the constant drift of the cash flows, σ_{OP} for their constant diffusion coefficient, Δt for the discrete length of the time increment and Z(t) denotes independent and identical standard-normally distributed variables at time t.

[123] See Flyvbjerg/Holm/Buhl (2003), p. 78.

[124] See Delegated Regulation (EU) 2016/467, article 1 (4, section 1, f (ii)).

[125] See, e.g., Jeong et al. (2016) or Ho/Liu (2002).

[126] See EIOPA (2014a), p. 16.

The parameters are calibrated using the empirical results found by Bitsch (2012) and Bahceci and Weisdorf (2014).[127] Therefore, the constant drift μ_{OP} is assumed to be 6 % and the constant diffusion coefficient σ_{OP} to be 7 % per annum. These values are also consistent with the level of those for the annualized returns of unlisted infrastructure assets provided by Table 4, indicating a range of 8 % to 14 % for the annual return and 4 % to 7 % for the annual volatility. Because those values are typically resulting from appraisal-based market values, they are not directly suitable for estimating the return and volatility behavior of the infrastructure asset's individual cash flows, but they provide suitable benchmarking values. The intended choice of a 6 % growth rate for the calibration of the operating cash flows` drift is indeed lower than the growth rate of the returns found in the literature, but it is still higher than the average GDP growth rate over the period 2010-2015 of 1.9 % in the OECD, that can be seen as an appropriate economically lower boundary condition.[128] Although this value for the drift in this setting might be lower than in reality, it is generally consistent with the condition that the introduction of a functional, i.e. necessary, infrastructure asset usually satisfies a prevailing unmet market demand and thus offers the potential of a cash flow growth rate higher than that for the general development of the economy. This condition seems to be reasonable, at least in the short-run, until general saturation effects on markets come into force that typically lower growth rates.

Regarding the diffusion coefficient for a direct infrastructure asset's operating cash flow, it seems to be reasonable to assess a level below that one applicable for a listed infrastructure asset. As mentioned by the literature, their valuations do not necessarily need to behave in the same manner, since there are distinct differences between the valuation cycles underlying both types of investments.[129] The comparison of the empirical volatilities for listed and unlisted infrastructure returns provided by Table 4 highlights that unlisted infrastructure returns are generally less volatile than that for listed assets.[130] Therefore, the intended value for the diffusion coefficient σ_{OP} of 7 % p.a. is below the general volatility level for listed infrastructure returns (Table 4) and hence seems to be reasonable.

The starting value of the operating cash flow, $CF^{OP}(0)$, is assumed to be 25 units of currency.

<u>Modeling decommissioning cash flows</u>

The cash flows for the decommissioning phase are also intended to follow the dynamics of the GBM due to its non-negativity condition and the absence of any mean reverting behavior. Their evolvement is illustrated by the equations (8) and (9).

$$dCF^{D}(t)=\mu_{D}CF^{D}(t)dt+\sigma_{D}CF^{D}(t)dW_{D}(t) \tag{8}$$

$$CF^{D}(t)=CF^{D}(t-1)\cdot\exp((\mu_{D}-\frac{\sigma_{D}^{2}}{2})\Delta t+\sigma_{D}\sqrt{\Delta t}Z(t)) \tag{9}$$

where: $CF^{D}(t)$ denotes the value of the decommissioning cash flows at time t, μ_{D} stands for the constant drift of the cash flows, σ_{D} for their constant diffusion coefficient, Δt for the discrete

[127] See Bitsch (2012), p. 210 and Bahceci/Weisdorf (2014), p. 34.

[128] See OECD (2016c), statistics about the GDP growth rate.

[129] See, for example, Humphreys/Maclean/Rogers (2016), p. 8.

[130] See AustralianSuper (2013), p. 3, for the investor's perspective on this issue.

length of the time increment and Z(t) denotes independent and identical standard-normally distributed variables at time t.

The main difference between the operating and decommission phase is the mature state of the asset's underlying business model. Since the asset's lifetime progressively expires, there are only a few remaining cash flows to realize. It is likely that the economic law of diminishing marginal utility also holds for the development of the market demand underlying the infrastructure asset's offered services. As the introduction of a functional infrastructure asset is usually subject to high cash flow growth rates caused by an increasing satisfaction of an unmet market demand at the beginning, it is likely that the asset is subject to increasing saturation effects when it matures. Because high cash flow growth rates typically attract competitors, the supply of similar services increases and thus, the marginal utility for consumers of the individual service offering shrinks. Hence, it can be expected that in the case of infrastructure assets, this condition will also hold, even if the barriers for market entries are usually high. In liberalized markets, it is likely that there are always some competitors entering the market, since it is also usually politically intended to avoid monopolistic market structures in the infrastructure sector. An illustrative example for this development can be found when considering the liberalization of the German long-distance traffic in 2013, which attracted several bus operators to compete for the profitable long-distance traffic of the Deutsche Bahn.

From an economic perspective, therefore, it can be expected that a future growth in the cash flows of an infrastructure asset subject to both, a relatively saturated market demand and a competitive market structure, can only be generated by a further growth of the whole economy, leading to a general increasing market demand for the offered service. The projected annual GDP growth rate of the OECD in 2017 is about 2 % and hence assumed to be a good approximation for the constant drift rate μ_D of the cash flows during the decommissioning phase in this setting.[131] By using a lower drift rate in comparison to the value used for the operating phase, this condition reflects a decline in the asset's market value for investors due to its transition of becoming a mature brownfield infrastructure asset.

The diffusion coefficient of this cash flow stream is assumed to be the same as for the operating phase, because it is not likely that there is a significant change in the underlying volatility condition for the market demand. Although there might be a higher competition in the market, leading to an increasing division of the total demand between all competitors, it is expected that this does not necessarily affect the cash flow stream's volatility, since the demand is considered to be both, relatively stable due to its general inelasticity and growing at least with the rate of the GDP.[132] Therefore, it is assumed that there is no change in the volatility of the infrastructure asset's cash flows during the transition from the operating into the decommissioning phase, leading to a diffusion coefficient σ_D of 7 %. The value of the first cash flow of the decommissioning phase, $CF^D(16)$, is based on the last cash flow from the operating phase, $CF^{OP}(15)$, in order to maintain a fluent transition between both phases.

[131] See OECD (2016c), statistics about the GDP growth rate.

[132] See, e.g., Inderst (2010), p. 73 or Newell/Peng (2008), p. 23.

Altogether, due to the fact that the cash flows stemming from the operating and decommissioning phase are non-negative by means of the GBM, the risk that an investment in this stylized infrastructure asset turns out to be worthless can only result from adverse construction costs scenarios. This condition is consistent with data provided by Moody's, showing that the construction phase is the most risky and adverse impact factor for the total performance of direct infrastructure assets (see chapter 2.1). Finally, due to the strictly positive cash flows from the operating and decommissioning phase, the model is consistent with the typical J-curve effect of cumulative infrastructure cash flows (see Figure 4).[133] From this point of view, the cumulative amount of cash flows starts to be negative at the beginning, since only construction costs exist, but begins to rise as positive cash flows are realizable and thus exhibits a shape similar to a J.

With regard to the second component of a DCF valuation model, the discount factor, assumptions on the term structure of interest rates are necessary. Basically, its value should reflect the risk-adjusted return requirement for the corresponding investor and hence be high enough in order to compensate the investor for the bearing of risks. Since it is assumed that all simulated infrastructure cash flows are totally realizable for the equity investor, their underlying risks are also entirely borne by the investor. Whereas the academic literature offers a vast number of theoretical approaches for determining an adequate and risk-adjusted return in general, empirical results for the case of infrastructure investments are still limited. In a recent article, Ammar and Eling (2015), for instance, introduce a nine-factor model in order to empirically explain the return behavior of listed infrastructure stocks.[134] However, for the sake of simplicity underlying this setting, and in order to focus on the dynamics of the infrastructure asset's cash flow streams, all of them are discounted by using the stochastic risk-free price of a default-free zero coupon bond at time t with maturity T, based on the stochastic interest rates provided by the model of Cox, Ingersoll and Ross (1985) (CIR-model).[135]

Modeling interest rates

The CIR-model determines the instantaneous and risk free short rate available at time t for an infinitesimally short period of time [t, t+dt) under the consideration of a mean reverting behavior. Based on these short rates, it is also possible to determine the whole term structure of the corresponding spot rates at time t for every maturity time T. The SDE of the relevant interest rate dynamics under the real-world condition are given by equation (10).[136]

$$dr(t)=[k\theta-(k+\lambda\sigma_r)r(t)]dt+\sigma_r\sqrt{r(t)}dW_r(t) \tag{10}$$

where: $dr(t)$ denotes the change in the short rate, k the constant speed of adjustment to the constant long-term mean value θ, λ the constant market price of risk, σ_r the constant value of volatility of the changes in the short rate, r(t) the instantaneous short rate at time t and $dW_r(t)$ a standard Wiener process (Brownian Motion).

133 See Gatzert/Kosub (2014), p. 353.

134 See Ammar/Eling (2015), p. 259.

135 See Cox/Ingersoll/Ross (1985).

136 See Brigo/Mercurio (2006), p. 65.

The first part of the SDE represents the drift term and hence the short rate's mean reverting behavior towards the long-term value θ, while the diffusion term ensures for the condition $2k\theta > \sigma_r^2$ that the short rate is strictly positive. The SDE can be discretized for simulation purposes using equation (11).[137]

$$r(t)=r(t-1)+k(\theta-r(t-1))\Delta t+\sigma_r\sqrt{\Delta t\cdot r(t-1)}Z(t) \tag{11}$$

where: $r(t)$ denotes the short rate at time t, k the constant speed of adjustment to the constant long-term mean value θ, σ_r the constant value of volatility of the changes in the short rate, Δt the discrete length of the time increment and Z(t) denotes independent and identical standard-normally distributed variables at time t. The parameters are calibrated by adjusting the annualized values given by Martin (2013), assuming that $k = 0.1036$, $\theta = 0.05$, $\sigma_r = 0.039$, $r(0) = 0.01$ and a market price of risk λ to be zero.[138] The short rate is calculated on a daily basis and transformed into annualized values using standard calculus.

Under this interest rate environment, there is an explicit solution for the price P(t,T) at time t of a default-free zero coupon bond paying one unit of currency at time T (maturity) given by equation (12).[139]

$$P(t,T)=A(t,T)\cdot\exp(-B(t,T)r(t)) \tag{12}$$

where

$$A(t,T)=\left[\frac{2h\cdot\exp[(k+h)(T-t)\cdot 0.5]}{2h+(k+h)\cdot(\exp[(T-t)h]-1)}\right]^{\frac{2k\theta}{\sigma_r^2}}$$

$$B(t,T)=\frac{2(\exp[(T-t)h]-1)}{2h+(k+h)\cdot(\exp[(T-t)h]-1)}$$

$$h=\sqrt{k^2+2\sigma_r^2}$$

When considering the infrastructure asset's cash flows as illustrated by Figure 3 in terms of individual default-free zero coupon bonds with maturity T denoting the point in time of their occurrence, and a face value equivalent to its cash flow value, their individual present values at each point in time t can be expressed by a function of P(t,T). Thereby, the present value at time t of an infrastructure asset's cash flow paying a certain amount of currency at time T should be consistent with the product of the cash flow's amount at time T multiplied by the current price P(t,T) of a default-free zero coupon bond, paying one unit of currency at the same maturity T under the CIR-model.

Since Solvency II requires a market oriented valuation of assets based on a true and fair view, a potential investor is willing to buy the infrastructure asset only for a fair value reflecting its future profit chance. Thus, the investor only values the asset's future and remaining cash flows that can be obtained from the asset. The present value of the infrastructure asset at time t can

[137] See Brigo et al. (2009), p. 398.

[138] See Martin (2013), p. 216.

[139] See Brigo/Mercurio (2006), p. 66.

hence be determined by equation (13) under consideration of the future and remaining cash flows at the valuation point in time t as follows.

$$PV(t) = -\sum_{T=1}^{l=3} C(T) \cdot P(t,T) + \sum_{T=4}^{m=15} CF^{OP}(T) \cdot P(t,T) + \sum_{T=16}^{n=20} CF^{D}(T) \cdot P(t,T) \quad (13)$$

where:

$$C(T) = \begin{cases} C(T), & T > t \\ 0, & T \leq t \end{cases}$$

$$CF^{OP}(T) = \begin{cases} CF^{OP}(T), & T > t \\ 0, & T \leq t \end{cases}$$

$$CF^{D}(T) = \begin{cases} CF^{D}(T), & T > t \\ 0, & T \leq t \end{cases}$$

where: PV(t) denotes the present value of the future and remaining cash flows from the asset at time t, C(T) the construction costs payable at time T, $CF^{OP}(T)$ the operating cash flows obtainable at time T, $CF^{D}(T)$ the decommissioning cash flows obtainable at time T, P(t,T) the present value of a default-free zero coupon bond paying one unit of currency at time T under the CIR-model. The respective future costs or cash flows applicable for the present value determination at time t are only considered if their maturity T is higher than the current point in time t (the valuation date).

4.1.2 Sensitivity analysis and findings

In order to assess the properties of the infrastructure model underlying this setting, the evolution of the infrastructure asset's value is simulated over time by means of a Monte Carlo simulation with 10 000 paths. An overview of all parameters used for the infrastructure asset's calibration of a base case scenario for the purpose of a sensitivity analysis is provided by Table 7. All Brownian motions underlying the stochastic processes of this setting, namely the infrastructure asset, the short rate and the other balance sheet items later explained in chapter 4.2, are correlated by coefficients summarized by Table 9 and by means of the Cholesky decomposition technique as explained in the Appendix A.1.

Table 7: Parameters applied for the calibration of the infrastructure asset's base case

Parameter	Calibration (p.a.)	Parameter	Calibration (p.a.)
Construction cost-multiple	2.0	σ_D	0.07
μ_C	0.04	r(0)	0.01
σ_C	0.10	Θ	0.05
μ_{OP}	0.06	σ_r	0.039
σ_{OP}	0.07	k	0.1036
μ_D	0.02	-	-

Source: Own table.

Unsurprisingly, the infrastructure model in this setting shows a strong sensitivity to the construction phase and its costs. The crucial point is the construction costs` multiple in relation to the first operating cash flow, because it works, depending on its magnitude, as a strengthening factor for the adverse effects of all other parameters used in this model. This typical behavior is especially disclosed when considering the evolution of the cumulative amount of cash flows that illustrates the common J-curve effect for infrastructure assets. Thereby, a higher multiple for the construction costs shifts the breakeven point at which the asset covers all of its expenses towards a longer period of time. In Figure 4, the doubling of the multiple leads to a shift for the breakeven point from time 8 to time 12, meaning that the construction costs consume a larger amount of the operating cash flows that cannot be realized by the investor.

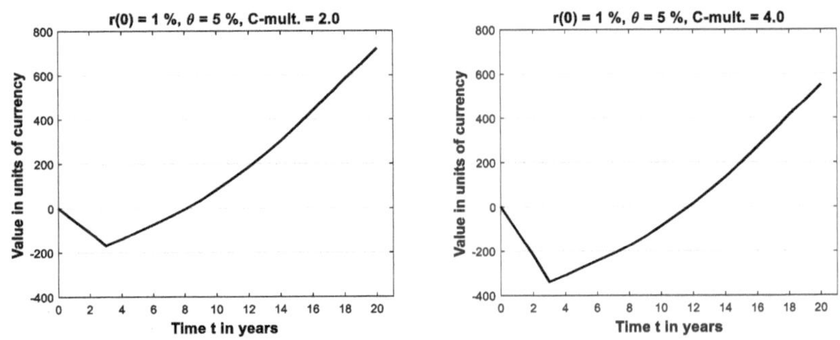

Figure 4: Two sample J-curve effects of the infrastructure asset´s cumulative cash flows (Source: Own figure).

In order to evaluate the effects of altering specific parameters on the asset´s performance and its risk contribution to the insurance company´s portfolio, two measures are chosen (Table 8). The probability of a negative net present value (P(N-NPV)) measures the probability that the infrastructure asset turns out to be an adverse investment decision and thus reflects the asset´s riskiness of drawing equity from the insurance company. Since the infrastructure asset typically varies its market value at every point in time due to the diminishing scope of the remaining cash flows, its performance needs to be assessed over the asset´s total lifespan. Therefore, the median over all simulated paths of the expected values of the asset´s individual present values from time zero to 20 ($Q_{0.5}(E^P[PV_{0\text{-}20}])$) is assumed to reflect the average performance of the asset over its lifetime.

Considering the effect of the level of the costs multiple, it can be concluded that the higher the multiple compared to the base case, the more adverse is the impact of the construction costs on the asset´s probability of providing a negative net present value for the insurance company and hence to draw equity. The same relationship is in effect for the median of the expected outcomes during the asset´s total lifespan. Therefore, the model is able to reflect the high riskiness of the construction phase according to data provided by Moody´s (see chapter 2.1) and underpins the phase´s strong influence on the overall performance of infrastructure assets in general.

Since the operating phase covers the longest time span of the infrastructure asset's lifetime, the model is very sensitive to changes in the calibration of the cash flows' growth factor and its diffusion term (μ_{OP} and σ_{OP}). A higher growth factor leads to a better performance in terms of higher amounts of cash flows which are more able to compensate the high losses due to the construction costs and thus leads to higher present values. By contrast, a higher diffusion coefficient leads to a higher probability of adverse scenarios of the cash flows' outcomes which finally worsen the asset's performance and raise the probability that the asset provides a negative net present value.

With regard to the interest rate environment, a higher long-term value θ leads to a higher probability of negative net present values depending on the level of the construction costs' multiple. The rationale is that the construction costs at the beginning of the asset's lifetime are discounted by higher discount factors than those used for the majority of cash flows arriving after the construction phase. Therefore, the adverse effect of the construction costs is intensified by higher and rising long-term interest rates and hence exerts a stronger influence on the asset's overall performance and its probability of providing a negative net present value.

Considering the starting value of the short rate's stochastic process, $r(0)$, the analysis shows that the asset's probability of providing a negative net present value is highly sensitive to this value. The higher the starting level compared to a fixed long-term value θ, the higher is the asset's potential to draw equity and the lower its median performance. The reason is that if a higher starting level at a given long-term value is chosen, the scope of cash flows that can be discounted by lower risk-free interest rates is diminishing and thus, the total present value shrinks.

Based on this setting, it can be concluded that infrastructure assets due to their commonly used valuation technique (DCF) are generally sensitive to changes in the interest rate environment and that this property provides an inherent source of risk which should be reflected in consideration of their regulatory treatment under Solvency II.

Table 8: Overview of the observed effects on the infrastructure asset

Measure \Variable	C-mult.	μ_C	σ_C	μ_{OP}	σ_{OP}	μ_D	σ_D	r(0)	Θ
P(N-NPV)	+ +	+	+	– –	+ +	–	+	+ +	+
$Q_{0.5}(E^P[PV_{0\text{-}20}])$	– –	–	–	+ +	– –	+	–	–	–

Source: Own table. + + stands for a strongly increasing effect, + for a lightly increasing effect, – for a lightly decreasing effect, – – for a strongly decreasing effect. C-mult. denotes the multiple for the construction costs in relation to the first operating cash flow. P(N-NPV) designates the probability of a negative net present value for the asset over all paths at time zero. $Q_{0.5}(E^P[PV_{0\text{-}20}])$ stands for the median of the expected values of all of the asset's present values from time zero to 20 over all paths.

4.2 Dynamics of the insurance company's balance sheet items

In order to evaluate the capital allocation, the riskiness and the performance of the insurance company's portfolio comprising an infrastructure asset, these questions need to be evaluated under consideration of the usual insurance balance sheet dynamics from the perspective of a market-oriented valuation. In this setting, the insurance company is able to invest its funds into two other assets available on the capital market. A risky asset (S) comprising stocks, whose market value is represented by the DAX under the dynamics of a GBM, and a risk-free asset (Bond), whose market value is represented by a money market account by means of the interest rate dynamics of the CIR-model. For completeness of the total balance sheet, the insurance company's liabilities are treated as a single item and assumed to follow a GBM for determining its market values.

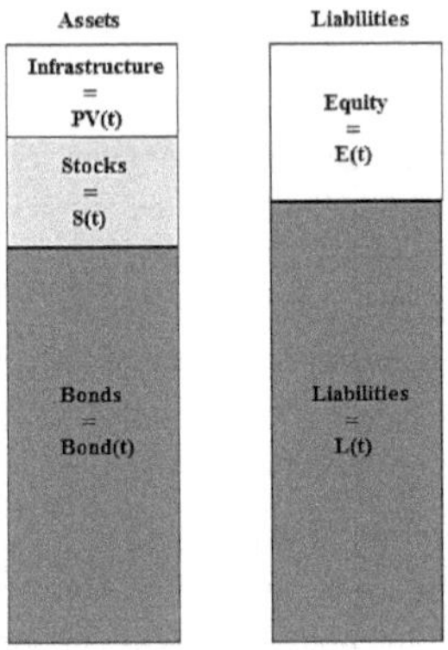

Figure 5: The insurance company's stylized balance sheet based on market values (Source: Own figure; based on time t).

Modeling the money market account

The risk-free asset is represented by a money market account which continuously realizes the corresponding risk-free rate as given by the CIR-model at every period t. This strategy is similar to a rolling over bond strategy, investing funds at every period t in a default-free zero coupon bond just maturing at time $t+\Delta t$. Due to its locally riskless investment behavior, this asset is assumed to be suitable for representing a risk-averse investment choice for the insurance company. Since the balance sheet is determined yearly, the interest rate r(t) is equal to the risk-free rate with a maturity of one year, r(t,1).

The underlying SDE is given by equation (14) with the discretized solution for this setting as given by equation (15).[140]

$$dBond(t)=Bond(t)r(t)dt \tag{14}$$

$$Bond(t)=Bond(t-1)\cdot\exp(r(t-1,1)\Delta t) \tag{15}$$

where: dBond(t) denotes the change in the value of the bank account, r(t) the short rate at time t for the period $[t, t+\Delta t)$ given by the CIR-model, Bond(t) the value of the bank account at time t, Δt the discrete time increment (one year) and r(t,1) the risk-free rate with a maturity of one year.

[140] See Brigo/Mercurio (2006), pp. 2-3 for equation (14). For small values of r(t), the approx. condition exp(r(t)) = 1+r(t) holds.

Modeling the risky asset

In order to supply the insurance company with an asset potentially realizing a yield above the risk-free rate, the insurance company is able to invest in a risky asset represented by the DAX. This asset is assumed to follow the dynamics of a GBM as given by equations (16) and (17).

$$dS(t)=\mu_S S(t)dt+\sigma_S(t)dW_S(t) \tag{16}$$

$$S(t)=S(t-1)\cdot\exp((\mu_S-\frac{{\sigma_S}^2}{2})\Delta t+\sigma_S\sqrt{\Delta t}Z(t)) \tag{17}$$

where: dS(t) denotes the change in the value of the risky asset, μ_S the constant drift, σ_S the constant diffusion coefficient, S(t) the value of the risky asset at time t, $dW_S(t)$ a standard Wiener process (Brownian Motion), Δt the discrete time increment and Z(t) denotes independent and identical standard-normally distributed variables at time t. The parameters are calibrated using monthly log-return data of the DAX during the period January 1991 until December 2015 (end of month values) and finally annualized using standard calculus as given in Appendix A.2.[141] The constant drift μ_S is 8 % and the constant volatility is 21 % per annum.

The starting values for the risk-free and risky assets´ processes, Bond(0) and S(0) respectively, are chosen such that the initial portfolio fraction of the infrastructure asset´s value at time zero, PV(0), amounts to 10 % of the total balance sheet´s value. This portfolio fraction is consistent with, for instance, the current proposal of a maximum threshold for infrastructure investments provided by the Norwegian Government Pension Fund Global.[142] The findings of Oyedele, Adair and McGreal (2014) underpin this threshold, since they show that a fraction of 10 % to 18 % for infrastructure investments is able to reduce the portfolio´s overall risk.[143]

Modeling the liabilities

In order to complete the design of the balance sheet dynamics, the market value of the insurance company´s liabilities is determined by using the approach of Fischer and Schlütter (2014). The liabilities are assumed to follow a GBM by means of equation (18) and in discretized form using equation (19).[144]

$$dL(t)=\mu_L L(t)dt+\sigma_L L(t)dW_L(t) \tag{18}$$

$$L(t)=L(t-1)\cdot\exp((\mu_L-\frac{{\sigma_L}^2}{2})\Delta t+\sigma_L\sqrt{\Delta t}Z(t)) \tag{19}$$

where: dL(t) denotes the change in the value of the liabilities, μ_L the constant drift, σ_L the constant diffusion coefficient, L(t) the value of the risky asset at time t, $dW_L(t)$ a standard Wiener process (Brownian Motion), Δt the time increment and Z(t) denotes independent and identical standard-normally distributed variables at time t. The parameters are calibrated by using the values given by Fischer and Schlütter (2014), leading to a constant drift μ_L of 1 % per

141 Data is retrieved from Yahoo! Finance.

142 See Nieuwerburgh et al. (2015), p. 6.

143 See Oyedele/Adair/McGreal (2014), p. 23.

144 See Fischer/Schlütter (2014), p. 9.

annum and a slightly adjusted constant volatility of 5 % per annum.[145] The starting value L(0) is calibrated with respect to the total value of the asset-side to represent a fraction of 80 %.

An overview of all parameters used for the calibration of the model is given in the Appendix A.3. Furthermore, the Brownian motions of all stochastic processes, i.e. for the infrastructure asset, the short rate, the risky asset and the liabilities, are correlated by coefficients summarized by Table 9 by means of the Cholesky decomposition technique as explained in the Appendix A.1. Due to the time-variant differences in their occurrence, the infrastructure asset's construction costs as well as both cash flow streams are not correlated with each other. All other correlation coefficients are mainly derived from the literature and it is assumed that their values are suitable for this setting.

Table 9: Correlation matrix used for the stochastic processes

	C	CF^{OP}	CF^{D}	Short rate r	Risky asset S	Liabilities L
C	1	-	-	-	-	-
CF^{OP}	0	1	-	-	-	-
CF^{D}	0	0	1	-	-	-
Short rate r	-0.15	-0.15	-0.15	1	-	-
Risky asset S	0.20	0.20	0.20	-0.15	1	-
Liabilities L	0	0	0	-0.25	-0.25	1

Source: Own table, coefficients based on: Table 5 for the correlation with the risky asset S; Fischer/Schlütter (2014), p. 12 for the liabilities; Niedrig (2015), p. 53 for the short rates.

4.3 Optimal asset allocation under solvency requirements

In order to investigate the performance of the insurance company's portfolio, the contribution of the infrastructure asset's performance to it and its interdependence with the dynamics of the other balance sheet items, the insurance company aims to maximize its net shareholder value under consideration of several constraints as explained in the following section.

4.3.1 Model framework under the VaR approach

At the beginning of its business at time t = 0, the insurance company is able to invest its initial funds into three asset classes: the risky stock (S), the risk-free money market account (Bond) similar to a rolling over one-year default-free zero bond strategy, and the illiquid infrastructure asset (I), leading to corresponding portfolio weights w_S, w_B, w_I. In Germany, insurance companies under Solvency II are no longer subject to the investment ordinance (AnlV), but are instead obliged to set up an internal investment catalog. Therefore, it is assumed that the portfolio weights for the model's setting are still to some extent aligned to the AnlV-quotes in order to maintain a certain level of safety.

145 See Fischer/Schlütter (2014), p. 12.

Thus, the initial weights for the base case scenario are set to $w_B = 72$ %, $w_S = 18$ % and $w_I = 10$ %.

It is assumed that the insurance company cannot rebalance its exposure to the infrastructure asset at any point in time, meaning that there is no drawing or investing of any additional funds to the infrastructure asset after its initiation at time zero. This is intended to reflect a specific portfolio constraint for investors in infrastructure assets, since the typical illiquidity of this kind of asset is usually causing a held to maturity approach due to the lack of valuable exit options or standardized secondary markets for trading infrastructure equity stakes.[146] However, from the viewpoint of the typical asset-liability-management approach of an insurance company, this held to maturity restriction does not necessarily imply a disadvantage compared to other assets as long as the infrastructure asset remains profitable and provides the insurance company with the ability to skim an adequate illiquidity premium.

The construction costs and the individual cash flows appear at the end of each year t and are immediately allocated to the funds that will be invested in the risk-free and risky asset over the next period t+1. For the case of construction costs, these draw equity from the insurance company at time t in terms of lowering the remaining funds allocatable to an investment in the risk-free and risky assets over the next period. This reflects the usually adverse impact of infrastructure costs on the asset's total performance and on the investor's solvency situation by causing the potential of a severe financial distress (see chapter 2.1). Since the operating and decommissioning cash flows are modeled to be strictly positive, their values in turn enhance the investment exposure in both assets over the following period.

The insurance company's total value of the asset-side at time t equals the sum of all assets currently held at time t. This value consists of the current values of the risky asset S(t), the risk-free asset Bond(t), the cash flow from the infrastructure asset CF(t) available for an investment in the risk-free or risky asset, or in case of the construction period, the construction costs C(t) reducing the total asset's value at time t, and the present value of the infrastructure asset's future and remaining cash flows at time t. The entire allocatable funds to the risk-free and risky asset for the next period are thus the total value of the asset-side at time t reduced by the infrastructure asset's present value due to its illiquidity. It is assumed that the insurance company immediately rebalances its portfolio with respect to its optimization function at the end of each year, so that both assets under their new portfolio fractions are able to realize their corresponding returns over the next period [t, t+Δt). Therefore, the insurance company's portfolio under the consideration that the infrastructure asset is held until maturity can be described as follows.

$$A(t)=S(t)+Bond(t)-C(t)+CF(t)+PV(t) \tag{20}$$

$$A^{alloc}(t)=A(t)-PV(t) = Bond^{adj}(t)+S^{adj}(t) \tag{21}$$

with

$$Bond^{adj}(t)=w_B \cdot A^{alloc}(t)$$

$$S^{adj}(t)=w_S \cdot A^{alloc}(t)$$

146 See Finkenzeller/Dechant/Schäfers (2010), p. 266.

This leads using equation (15) and (17) to the portfolio's total value of the asset-side at time t+1 as follows.

$$\mathrm{Bond}(t+1)=\mathrm{Bond}^{adj}(t)\cdot\exp(r(t,1)\Delta t) \tag{22}$$

$$S(t+1)=S^{adj}(t)\cdot\exp((\mu_S-\frac{\sigma_S^2}{2})\Delta t+\sigma_S\sqrt{\Delta t}Z(t+1)) \tag{23}$$

$$A(t+1)=S(t+1)+\mathrm{Bond}(t+1)-C(t+1)+CF(t+1)+PV(t+1) \tag{24}$$

where: A(t) denotes the total asset value at time t, consisting of S(t), meaning the value of the risky asset at time t, Bond(t), denotes the value of the risk-free asset at time t, CF(t) stands for the cash flow obtained at time t = T (its maturity), C(t) for the costs payable at time t = T if $t \leq 3$ (last period for construction costs), PV(t) denotes the present value of the infrastructure asset's future and remaining cash flows at time t, $A^{alloc}(t)$ the allocatable funds at time t for rebalancing purposes over the next period [t, t+Δt), $\mathrm{Bond}^{adj}(t)$ and $S^{adj}(t)$ stand for the rebalanced values of the risk-free and risky asset at time t that realize their respective returns over the next period [t, t+Δt), Δt for the discrete time increment (one year), r(t,1) for the one-year risk-free short rate, w_B and w_S for the weights of the risk-free and risky asset, respectively.

At the end of each year t, just after realizing the infrastructure asset's costs or cash flows, the insurance company can only decide on the optimal portfolio weights for the stocks and bond asset over the following period due to the infrastructure asset's illiquidity. The weights w_S and w_B are chosen under consideration of the regulatory constraints given by Solvency II in terms of a maximum permitted probability of insolvency of less than 0.5 % over a one-year horizon. The insurance company thus optimizes its one-year ahead investment strategy in this setting by adopting the approach described by Niedrig (2015). Thereby, the insurance company maximizes its one-year net shareholder value (NSHV) through choosing the adequate portfolio weights for stocks and bonds.[147] Therefore, from time t = 1 until T = 19, the insurance company optimizes its portfolio according to the following function:

$$\mathrm{NSHV}(t)=\max_{w_S,w_B}\{\exp(-r(t,1))\cdot E^P[\max\{A(t+1)-L(t+1);0\}-[A(t)-L(t)]]\} \tag{25}$$

subject to:

$$w_S+w_B=1 \tag{26}$$

$$w_B\in[\max(w_B^{unadj}-\delta;\ w_B^{min});\ \min(w_B^{unadj}+\delta;\ 1)] \tag{27}$$

$$P\{A(t+1)<L(t+1)\}\leq 1-\alpha \tag{28}$$

where: NSHV(t) denotes the net shareholder value at time t, $w_{S,B}$ the portfolio weights for the stocks or bond investment at time t, r(t,1) the one-year risk-free rate given by the CIR-model, A(t) the value of the total assets at time t, L(t) the value of the liabilities at time t+1, δ the maximum permitted change in the portfolio weights of the risk-free and risky asset, w_B^{min} the minimum portfolio weight of the risk-free asset according to the insurance company's internal investment catalog (70 %), w_B^{unadj} the portfolio weight of the risk-free asset before adjustment,

[147] See Niedrig (2015), p. 46.

P the probability function and α stands for the required confidence interval (99.5 %) of Solvency II. The expression A(t)-L(t) determines the value of the equity capital at time t.

The first constraint (26) can be seen as both, a budget and illiquidity constraint, which ensures that the allocatable funds are entirely invested into the risk-free and risky asset over the next period. The second constraint (27) allows the insurance company to change the portfolio weights for the risk-free and risky assets by only a maximum of $\delta = 20$ % each period according to its unadjusted value.[148] Due to the implementation of a minimum weight for the risk-free asset (w_B^{min}), it also comprises a short sale constraint that prevents the insurance company to short sale any stocks or to borrow money in case of the risk-free asset. Simultaneously, it requires the weights regarding the allocatable funds to permanently stay within a range given by the internal investment catalog, assumed as $w_B \in [0.70; 1], w_S \in [0; 0.30]$, in order to reflect a conservative and risk-averse investment approach. The last constraint (28) describes the solvency requirement introduced by Solvency II and technically ensures that the insurance company will be solvent in 99.5 % of all cases over one year (confidence level of 99.5 %), since insolvency is technically expressed as a lower value of total assets compared to liabilities at time t+1, namely $A(t+1) < L(t+1)$. Finally, it is assumed that the capital market for the risk-free and risky assets is liquid and that there are no trading costs.

The regulatory solvency capital requirement is defined as the VaR of the change in the basic own funds at a confidence level of 99.5 % and can be determined as the smallest amount x for which equation (29) holds.[149] After choosing the optimal portfolio weights for the assets, its value is equivalent to the 99.5 percentile of the loss distribution of the optimal portfolio strategy over one year.

$$SCR(t)^{VaR} := \underset{x}{\operatorname{argmin}} \{P\{A(t)\text{-}L(t)\text{-}\exp(-r(t,1))\cdot[A(t+1)\text{-}L(t+1)] > x\} \leq 1\text{-}\alpha\} \qquad (29)$$

where: $SCR(t)^{VaR}$ denotes the solvency capital requirement at time t based on the VaR approach, P the probability function, A(t) the value of the total assets at time t, L(t) the value of the liabilities at time t, r(t,1) the one-year risk-free rate at time t as given by the CIR-model and α stands for the confidence interval (99.5 %). The expression within the probability function is defined as the loss variable.

This value technically ensures that the probability of a loss over one year exceeding the SCR is less or equal to 0.5 %. The risk margin is excluded in this calculation of the SCR as this would otherwise lead to a circular problem, since the risk margin, SCR and the regulatory available equity capital, are depending on each other. Thus, the change in the available equity capital is approximated by the change in the basic own funds as expressed by the change in the net asset value.[150] Finally, the capital market is projected over 20 years with 10 000 paths. At the end of each year, 10 000 outcomes of the one-year strategie for each portfolio combination are projected in order to assess the best portfolio choice.

148 See Niedrig (2015), p. 53.

149 See Börger (2010), p. 229 or Christiansen/Niemeyer (2012), p. 4.

150 See Börger (2010), p. 229.

All parameters applied in the analysis are summarized by the Appendix A.3 and represent the setting's base case. Different levels of the parameters are finally used for a sensitivity analysis and the results are shown in the analysis section in chapter 4.3.3.

4.3.2 Solvency capital requirements using the Solvency II standard formula

The optimal SCR at time t based on the VaR approach is compared to the SCR by means of the standard formula of Solvency II in order to detect any deviation and its magnitude. Since the standard formula is developed to be applicable for every insurance company, it is likely that its SCR overestimates that one determined by a tailored VaR approach. This expected deviation is thus a driving force for identifying a potentially better fitting capital charge for the infrastructure asset under the standard formula in order to narrow that potential gap (chapter 4.4).

The underlying setting concentrates only on the capital requirements resulting from the market risk module as this exhibits to be the most important one for insurance companies based on the latest QIS 5 impact study.[151] The market risk module is intended to cover risks stemming from changes in the level or volatility of market prices for financial assets held by the insurance company.[152] Thereby, it comprises the portfolio's risk measured by its exposure to certain risks regarding several sub-modules, like the interest rate risk, equity risk, property risk, spread risk, currency risk and concentration risk.[153] For the sake of simplicity, and in accordance to the insurance company's balance sheet items as outlined in chapter 4.2 as well as to approaches commonly used in the literature, several sub-modules are excluded from further analysis.[154] Property risk is excluded, since the insurance company does not invest into property assets. Spread risk is excluded, because the risk-free asset in this setting can be considered as a revolving default-free zero bond strategy similar to investments in one-year maturing AAA-graded EEA government bonds, which are currently neither considered in the spread risk nor in the concentration risk sub-module.[155] Currency risk is treated as perfectly hedged. Concentration risk is considered to be negligible due to the portfolio's alignment to a well-diversified internal investment catalog in practice and the absence of a mandatory treatment of government bonds in this module. However, it is worth noting that direct infrastructure assets typically need large capital commitments, so that concentration risks comprised by this sub-module should be apparent in practice. Furthermore, the calculations are based on neglecting the symmetric adjustment mechanism.

[151] See EIOPA (2011), p. 65.

[152] See EIOPA (2014a), p. 13.

[153] See Delegated Regulation (EU) 2015/35, section 5, subsection 1 (164).

[154] See, e.g. Niedrig/Gründl (2015), pp. 10-11.

[155] See ESRB (2015), p. 33.

The overall SCR for the market risk is determined by aggregating the underlying risk sub-modules under consideration of diversification effects as follows.[156]

$$SCR_{mkt}^{S\,II}(t)=\sqrt{\sum_{i,j} Corr_{i,j}\cdot SCR_i(t)\cdot SCR_j(t)} \quad (30)$$

where: $SCR_{mkt}^{S\,II}(t)$ denotes the total solvency capital requirement at time t for the market risk module using the standard formula, $Corr_{i,j}$ the predetermined correlation coefficients for sub-modules i and j and $SCR_{i,j}(t)$ the capital requirements for sub-modules i and j. The correlation matrix is given in Appendix A.4.

The calculation of the solvency capital requirements for each sub-module is based on changes in the basic own funds as expressed by instantaneous changes in the net asset value resulting from predefined shock scenarios. The change in the net asset value is defined as the change in the market values of all assets and liabilities that are sensitive to the considered risk source before and after applying the corresponding shock factor. Its calculation thus takes the whole balance sheet dynamics into account when applying a given shock scenario. However, the approach often used in literature for calculating the changes in the net asset value focuses only on changes in the market values of the risk's directly underlying asset class. Hence, it neglects any corresponding simultaneous changes in the values of the other remaining asset classes and the liabilities of the balance sheet due to this shock scenario.[157] Thereby, the approach considers the change in the market values of an asset class due to the applied shock scenario as equivalent to the change in the net asset value and thus, as equal to the expected capital loss for the solvency requirements. This concept is to some extent biasing, since it disentangles economic interdependencies, especially between assets and liabilities that might mitigate the capital loss.

However, neglecting such interdependencies seems to be currently the only adequate approach due to the lack of suitable estimating techniques that are able to properly approximate the respective simultaneous changes in the market values of the other balance sheet items that are sensitive to the corresponding risk scenario. Therefore, it is assumed for the following determination of the SCRs for the interest rate risk and equity risk sub-modules that each applied shock scenario only affects the market value of the underlying individual asset class and the capital requirement is thus approximated by equation (31).[158] Furthermore, since it is assumed that the insurance company optimizes its portfolio immediately at the end of each year t, the determination of the SCR is based on the optimized closing balance sheet at time t, which is equivalent to the opening balance sheet at time t+1.

$$\Delta NAV=\max[NAV-(NAV|shock);0]=\max[A-L-((A-L)|shock);0]=\max[A-(A|shock);0] \quad (31)$$

where: ΔNAV denotes the difference in the net asset value before and after applying a shock scenario, NAV stands for the net asset value in terms of the difference in the market values of assets (A) and liabilities (L).

156 See Delegated Regulation (EU) 2015/35, section 5, subsection 1 (164).

157 See, e.g., Gatzert/Martin (2012), p.7.

158 See Gatzert/Martin (2012), p.7.

The interest rate risk sub-module

This sub-module is intended to capture the risk of changes in the market value of assets and liabilities resulting from changes in the term structure of interest rates. The approach assumes an instantaneous increase or decrease of the basic-risk free rate for each maturity based on predefined shock scenarios. The required capital for the upward or downward movement of interest rates is determined by the change in the net asset value due to revaluation of all sensitive exposures under an altered term structure. The final capital requirement for the sub-module is the maximum capital requirement of both shift scenarios.

The altered term structure is derived by multiplying the current interest rate by the growth or decline factor according to the shock scenario. The increase of interest rates should be at least one percentage point at any maturity.[159]

$$r_{u/d}(t) = r(t) \cdot (1+s_{u/d}) \tag{32}$$

where: $r_{u/d}(t)$ denotes the interest rate after the corresponding upward (u) or downward (d) shock for maturity t, r(t) the current interest rate before the shock and $s_{u/d}$ the predefined factors for the upward (u) or downward (d) shock scenarios per maturity t.

For the setting of the insurance company's balance sheet, only the risk of an upward shift in the term structure of interest rates is able to draw any equity due to losses from the asset-side in terms of the risk-free asset. With regard to the liability-side, only the downward shock scenario can consume any equity capital and thus endanger the insurance company's solvency situation.

Since the insurance company holds on the asset-side only a risk-free asset depending on the interest rate, i.e. the stochastic one-year short rate, its solvency capital requirement can be calculated as the loss in its present values due to an altered one-year interest rate. Using equation (22), the present value of the risk-free asset at the beginning of period t equals the risk-free asset's fund value after its optimization at the end of the previous period t-1. In order to capture the instantaneous loss due to the altered interest rate, the stressed present value of the risk-free asset at time t equals the market value of the risk-free asset at time t+1 when realizing its return over the one-year horizon under the CIR-model, but discounted back to time t with the altered one-year interest rate. The capital loss is thus the difference between both present values at time t (equation (33)).

$$SCR^{u}_{int}(t) = NAV(t) - NAV_u(t) = PV(t) - PV_u(t) \tag{33}$$

with

$$PV(t) = Bond^{adj}(t-1) \tag{34}$$

$$PV_u(t) = [Bond^{adj}(t-1) \cdot \exp(r(t)\Delta t)] \cdot \exp(-r_u(t)\Delta t) \tag{35}$$

where: $SCR^{u}_{int}(t)$ denotes the solvency capital requirement for the interest rate risk in the upward shock scenario, NAV(t) the net asset value at time t, $NAV_u(t)$ the net asset value at time t under the upward shock scenario, PV(t) the present value of the risk-free asset at time t, $Bond^{adj}(t)$

159 See EIOPA (2014b), p. 143 and Delegated Regulation (EU) 2015/35, section 5, subsec. 2 (166). For the upward scenario, due to the 1 % change requirement, the calculation actually specifies to $r_u(t) = \max[(r(t) \cdot (1+s_u); r(t)+1\,\%]$.

the optimized risk-free asset's value at time t, $PV_u(t)$ the present value of the risk-free asset under the upward shock scenario, r(t) the one-year short rate given by the CIR-model and $r_u(t)$ the altered short rate under the upward scenario. Since the risk-free asset depends on the one-year short rate, its corresponding shock factor s_u is equivalent to an increase of 70 %.[160]

Due to the fact that the technical provisions of an insurance company are sensitive to changes in the risk-free rate in practice, the liabilities in this setting are also assumed to show a similar relationship. Therefore, the potential loss in equity is approximated by the changes in the market values of the liabilities resulting from discounting them by means of the altered one-year interest rate (equation (36)).

$$SCR_{int}^{d}(t)=NAV(t)\text{-}NAV_d(t)=PV_d(t)\text{-}PV(t) \quad (36)$$

with

$$PV(t)=L(t+1)\cdot\exp(-r(t)\Delta t) \quad (37)$$

$$PV_d(t)=L(t+1)\cdot\exp(-r_d(t)\Delta t) \quad (38)$$

where: $SCR_{int}^{d}(t)$ denotes the solvency capital requirement for the interest rate risk in the downward shock scenario, NAV(t) the net asset value at time t, $NAV_d(t)$ the net asset value at time t under the downward shock scenario, PV(t) the present value of the liabilities at time t, L(t) the value of the liabilities at time t, $PV_d(t)$ the present value of the liabilities under the downward shock scenario, r(t) the short rate given by the CIR-model and $r_d(t)$ the altered short rate under the downward scenario. Since the discounting period depends on the one-year short rate, its corresponding shock factor s_d is equivalent to a decrease of 75 %.[161]

As mentioned in section 3.2, the appropriateness of a regulatory treatment of the infrastructure asset within the interest rate risk sub-module remains still unclear. The present value of the infrastructure asset in this setting is determined as the sum of all present values of the asset's remaining and future cash flows based on a discounted cash flow approach. This calculation depends heavily on the risk-free short rate provided by the CIR-model as shown in chapter 4.1.1 and thus, any shift in the term structure of interest rates leads automatically to a change in the asset's total market value. This raises the question whether the infrastructure equity investment needs to be taken into account within the interest rate sub-module. In this context, the regulation generally stipulates that a discounted value of future cash flows is exposed to the interest rate risk.[162] Nevertheless, it simultaneously states that equity investments as well as direct property investments should not be considered as sensitive to changes in the term structure of interest rates and hence do not need to be considered in this sub-module.[163] Because the guidelines on the treatment of the market risk exposure provided by EIOPA (2015b) suggest to apply that sub-module which corresponds to the asset's predominant economic characteristic, it does not

[160] See Delegated Regulation (EU) 2015/35, section 5, subsection 2 (166).

[161] See Delegated Regulation (EU) 2015/35, section 5, subsection 2 (167).

[162] See EIOPA (2014b), p. 141, SCR 5.20.

[163] See EIOPA (2014b), p. 141, SCR 5.18.

stipulate a comparison of the asset´s solvency requirements in both sub-modules and to take the higher capital requirement.[164]

In order to get a first insight into the risk of potential equity losses due to an altered interest rate term structure applicable for infrastructure assets, the stressed present values of the infrastructure asset in this setting are calculated and its solvency capital requirement for a treatment under the interest rate risk sub-module is determined. For this purpose, the corresponding spot rate curve for the maturities 1 to 20 is determined at every period t based on the short rates provided by the CIR-model (equation (12)) and finally stressed by the upward shock scenario, because the infrastructure asset is on the asset-side.[165] The resulting solvency capital requirement for the infrastructure asset exposed to the interest rate risk is the difference between the unstressed and the stressed present value as generally provided by equation (33).

The equity risk sub-module

The equity risk sub-module measures the risk arising from an instantaneous drop in the market values of equities according to a predefined shock scenario. It currently distinguishes between three classes of equities, namely type 1 equities, comprising equities listed in regulated markets in the EEA or OECD, type 2 equities, covering equities not listed in the EEA or OECD, unlisted equities, commodities and other alternative investments, and qualifying infrastructure equities, incorporating infrastructure SPV investments which need to fulfill specific qualifying criteria as outlined in chapter 3.2.[166] The corresponding different treatments of the underlying capital charges in case of non-strategic investments are summarized by Table 6, the main rationale of this sub-risk module is also explained in chapter 3.2. The solvency capital requirement for the equity risk sub-module can be determined by means of equation (2) for every period t as follows.

$$SCR_{equ}(t)=\sqrt{SCR^2_{type\,1}(t)+2\cdot 0.75\cdot SCR_{type\,1}(t)\cdot\left(SCR_{type\,2}(t)+SCR_{qinf}(t)\right)+\left(SCR_{type\,2}(t)+SCR_{qinf}(t)\right)^2} \quad (39)$$

For the setting of the underlying model, the insurance company holds a risky asset S represented by an investment in the DAX and thus, this exposure needs to be considered as type 1 equity. For the infrastructure asset, all three possible cases are considered in order to cover the whole scope of possible risk charges for infrastructure equity investments, i.e. treating it either to be a type 2 equity (49 % shock), a qualifying infrastructure investment in terms of a SPV (30 % shock) or a qualifying infrastructure investment in terms of a corporate structure (36 % shock). Furthermore, it is assumed that the qualifying criteria are met and that the SCR for qualifying corporates just replaces the SCR for qualifying SPV in equation (39).

The individual solvency capital requirements for the different equity classes in this setting are determined as follows.[167] The capital loss equals the instantaneous decline in the market values at time t of the risky asset S by considering the shock application on its optimized portfolio

[164] See EIOPA (2015b), guideline 5.

[165] See Björk (2009), p. 352 for the formula of continuous spot rates.

[166] See Delegated Regulation (EU) 2015/35, article 168 (1-3) and Delegated Regulation (EU) 2016/467, article 1 (4, section 5).

[167] See EIOPA (2014b), p. 146, SCR 5.42.

fraction at the end of the previous period t-1. For the infrastructure asset, the capital loss equals a decrease of its present value at time t due to the shock scenario.

$$SCR_{equ,i}(t)=\max[(\Delta NAV(t)|\text{equity shock}_i);0] \tag{40}$$

with

$$SCR_{type\ 1}(t)=\max[S^{adj}(t\text{-}1)\text{-}\{S^{adj}(t\text{-}1)\cdot(1\text{-}0.39)\};0] \tag{41}$$

$$SCR_{inf}(t)=\max[PV(t)\text{-}\{PV(t)\cdot(1\text{-}s_{infra,j})\};0] \tag{42}$$

where: $SCR_{equ,i}(t)$ denotes the solvency capital requirement for the equity risk of equity class i (type 1, type 2, qualifying infrastructure), $\Delta NAV(t)$ the change in the net asset value at time t based on the optimized asset's value for the risky asset S and the current present value PV(t) for the infrastructure asset, equity shock_i stands for the application of the corresponding shock factor for equity class i, $SCR_{type\ 1}(t)$ denotes the solvency capital requirement for the risky asset S at time t, $S^{adj}(t)$ the optimized portfolio fraction of the risky asset S at time t and $s_{infra,j}$ stands for one of the three possible risk charges j applicable for infrastructure equity investments (Table 6).

Finally, the total market solvency capital requirement under consideration of diversification benefits between the equity and interest risk can be determined based on equation (30) as follows.

$$SCR_{mkt}^{S\ II}(t)=\sqrt{\sum_{int,equ} Corr_{int,equ}\cdot SCR_{int}(t)\cdot SCR_{equ}(t)} \tag{43}$$

where: $SCR_{mkt}^{S\ II}(t)$ denotes the solvency capital requirement at time t for the market risk under the standard formula of Solvency II, $Corr_{int,equ}$ the correlation matrix between the solvency capital requirements of the interest rate risk and equity risk sub-module as specified in the Appendix A.4, $SCR_{int,equ}$ the solvency capital requirements for the interest rate risk and equity risk sub-module.

4.3.3 Analysis and findings

For the calibration of a base case scenario for the insurance company's portfolio maximizing the net shareholder value when comprising an infrastructure asset, the parameters provided in Table 10 are applied.

Table 10: Parameters applied for the calibration of the portfolio´s base case

Parameter	Calibration (p.a.)	Parameter	Calibration (p.a.)
Construction cost-multiple	2.0	r(0)	0.01
μ_C	0.04	Θ	0.05
σ_C	0.10	σ_r	0.039
μ_{OP}	0.06	k	0.1036
σ_{OP}	0.07	$w_{B(0)}$	0.72
μ_D	0.02	$w_{S(0)}$	0.18
σ_D	0.07	$w_{I(0)}$	0.10
μ_S	0.08	$w_{L(0)}$	0.80
σ_S	0.21	δ	0.20
μ_L	0.01	w_B^{min}	0.70
σ_L	0.05	w_S^{max}	0.30

Source: Own table.

Table 11 shows the time-variant evolution of the portfolio maximizing the net shareholder value for the base case scenario. Due to the illiquidity constraint and the resulting non-adjustment of the infrastructure asset´s stake, its portfolio fraction increases only until the end of the construction phase (period 3), since the stream of construction costs that lowers the asset´s present value continuously shrinks. After period 5, the insurance company begins to shift its portfolio progressively into the risky asset.

The portfolio´s overall level of risk according to the optimal portfolio weights is analyzed by means of two ratios. The solvency ratio is measured as the ratio between the insurance company´s own funds at time t and the one-year ahead solvency capital requirement using the VaR approach. The SCR-fraction is determined as the ratio of the solvency capital requirement to the portfolio´s total asset value at time t.[168] Unsurprisingly, with regard to the lifecycle stages of the infrastructure asset, its construction phase denotes the most riskiest period of time indicated by the lowest solvency ratios in conjunction with the highest fractions of the portfolio´s solvency capital requirement. This behavior is mainly caused by two channels. First, the construction costs of the infrastructure asset directly draw equity capital in terms of lowering the insurance company´s funds allocatable to the risk-free and risky asset funds for the next period. Furthermore, the infrastructure asset´s present value continuously grows during the construction phase, since a stream of costs for the investor drops out at every period. Both properties endanger the company´s solvency situation through tightening its funds remaining for future investment purposes and hence hindering its ability to generate sufficient returns in order to meet its obligations in terms of the liabilities one year ahead. Since the insurance company is also subject to both, a weight and a solvency constraint, it is not permitted to increase the risky asset´s fraction in an unlimited manner in order to gamble for meeting its liabilities. Nevertheless, because the risk-free asset only realizes a low return due to the

168 Solvency ratio: $\frac{E^P[E(t)]}{SCR(t)^{VaR}}$. SCR-fraction: $\frac{SCR(t)^{VaR}}{E^P[A(t)]}$.

implemented low interest rate environment (1 %), the company is forced to lower its stake in the risk-free asset towards its minimum weight, in order to increase its potential for realizing a higher portfolio return through higher stakes in the risky asset as long as allowed by the constraints.

Table 11: The insurance company´s optimized portfolio for the base case scenario

Time t	**0**	**1**	**2**	**3**	**4**	**5**	**6**	**7**	**8**	**9**	**10**	**11**	**12**	**13**	**14**	**15**	**16**	**17**	**18**	**19**	**20**
w_B	0,7200	0,7002	0,7007	0,7154	0,8479	0,8647	0,7663	0,7549	0,7002	0,7009	0,7004	0,7008	0,7000	0,7001	0,7000	0,7008	0,7002	0,7002	0,7008	0,7001	0,6935
w_S	0,1800	0,1861	0,1719	0,1434	0,0191	0,0096	0,1155	0,1353	0,1986	0,2070	0,2163	0,2249	0,2346	0,2434	0,2524	0,2605	0,2696	0,2777	0,2848	0,2929	0,2996
w_I	0,1000	0,1137	0,1274	0,1412	0,1330	0,1257	0,1182	0,1098	0,1011	0,0922	0,0833	0,0743	0,0654	0,0565	0,0476	0,0387	0,0302	0,0221	0,0144	0,0070	0,0069
S-ratio	1,22	1,29	1,49	1,87	2,63	2,63	2,52	2,57	2,41	2,55	2,74	2,97	2,95	3,01	3,12	3,25	3,23	3,40	3,49	3,55	-
SCR	0,16	0,16	0,15	0,13	0,10	0,10	0,11	0,12	0,14	0,14	0,14	0,14	0,14	0,15	0,15	0,15	0,16	0,16	0,16	0,16	-

Source: Own table. w_B, w_S and w_I stand for the risk-free, risky and infrastructure assets´ weights, respectively. S-ratio denotes the solvency ratio and SCR the fraction of the solvency capital requirement in relation to the portfolio´s value.

This special situation stemming from the interaction between the illiquidity, weight and solvency constraints with the equity-consuming characteristic of the construction phase, is underpinned by Table 12. It shows a clearly and consistently higher multiple of the risk-free asset´s average weight in relation to the risky asset´s average weight when compared to the other lifecycle phases of the infrastructure asset. On the one hand, it indicates the investor´s general preference for a less risky portfolio composition. However, it also illustrates that if the investor is exposed to a higher infrastructure asset´s initial portfolio weight, the portfolio´s composition shifts more strongly towards the risky asset during the construction phase in order to get compensated for the higher losses in equity due to the stronger adverse effect of the construction costs. This incentive for choosing a riskier portfolio composition provides the second channel of risk during the portfolio´s early lifespan that is able to endanger the insurance company´s overall solvency situation.

After overcoming the construction phase at period 4, the solvency ratio as well as the fraction of the solvency capital requirement instantaneously improve. This general development is only interrupted for a short period of time due to adverse scenarios for the risky asset and the liabilities at periods 4 and 5, which put the company´s equity stake under strong pressure. Since the insurance company is still in a low interest rate environment, its equity position is not resilient enough to compensate the risks and losses stemming from the risky asset. Thus, it is forced to shift its funds almost totally into the risk-free asset in order to fulfill the default probability implemented by the solvency constraint. However, for the case of lower initial weights for the risky asset, this strong shift considerably mitigates, since the magnitude of potential losses also declines.

However, the insurance company thereafter benefits from the stable and continuous cash flow generation of the infrastructure asset and is able to progressively increase its funds into the risky asset in order to raise the portfolio's net shareholder value while limiting the portfolio's risk. In this regard, the results of a sensitivity analysis provided by Table 13 highlight the asset's positive influence on the portfolio's default probability and its solvency ratio. The infrastructure asset's stable cash flow provision exerts a kind of risk mitigating effect by strengthening the portfolio's general resilience against the potential of higher losses when increasing the exposure to the risky asset. This effect can be underpinned by the findings of Oyedele, Adair and McGreal (2014), who show that the allocation of funds to infrastructure assets leads to a strong benefit in terms of the portfolio's risk situation.[169]

At the end of the insurance company's investment horizon, the portfolio weights are almost totally shifted close to their individual boundary conditions, i.e. 70 % for the risk-free asset and 30 % for the risky asset as the maximum allowed weight. Simultaneously, the solvency ratio reaches its maximum.

Table 12: Risk-free to risky asset multiples for different infrastructure weights

Phase \ Initial infrastructure	0.005	0.01	0.02	0.04	0.06	0.10
Construction phase	5,4	5,4	5,3	4,9	4,7	4,3
Operating phase	1,8	1,8	1,8	1,8	1,9	2,0
Decommissioning phase	1,5	1,5	1,5	1,5	1,5	1,6

Source: Own table. The average weight of the risk-free asset is divided by the average weight of the risky asset for each phase of the infrastructure asset's lifecycle.

Considering the observed sensitivity effects of the portfolio based on the base case scenario (Table 13), the most influential parameters are the construction costs' multiple, the operating cash flows' drift term, the initial portfolio's fraction of the infrastructure asset and the starting value of the short rate's stochastic process. The rationales behind the working channels of all parameters except for the infrastructure asset's weight are already explained in chapter 4.1.2.

The sensitivity analysis of the infrastructure asset's initial portfolio weight, $w_I(0)$, points out a trade-off situation for the insurance company between the portfolio's gain in the net shareholder value and its riskiness. Thereby, a higher weight leads to a generally stronger effect of the asset's underlying illiquidity constraint, which emerges in a stronger limitation of the optimal weights for the risky asset compared to the base case. Because there are less funds allocatable to the risky asset over the remaining time, the portfolio's potential to realize higher returns and to achieve higher net shareholder values is, consequently, generally restricted.

The working mechanism of the illiquidity constraint, however, clearly emerges when comparing the portfolio comprising the infrastructure asset to a portfolio only consisting of the

169 See Oyedele/Adair/McGreal (2014), p. 23.

risk-free and risky asset, but also subject to the same weights, parameters and objective function. In this setting, the illiquidity constraint in the infrastructure portfolio leads to an average underfunding of the risky asset of 5.6 % over the total period of 20 years. However, considering the evolution of the risky asset's weights in both portfolios, their differences tend to decrease towards the end of the total investment horizon as the infrastructure weights continuously shrink and the resulting illiquidity constraint loses its power. At the end, the weights of the risky assets in both portfolios converge to their maximum bound allowed by the portfolio's weight constraint. Consequently, the net shareholder value is on average 7.6 % lower than that for the portfolio without the infrastructure asset, which is mainly caused by the significant differences in the risky asset's exposure at the portfolio's early periods.

With regard to the portfolios' riskiness, however, the infrastructure portfolio behaves significantly less risky. Its average default probability amounts to the half of the two-asset portfolio, its average solvency ratio is 12.8 % larger and the average SCR-fraction 20.4 % lower. This leads to the conclusion that the illiquidity constraint of the infrastructure asset plays a significant role for a portfolio's performance in terms of its risk-return profile at least based on this setting, since it slows down the increase in the exposure to the risky asset and thus improves the portfolio's overall riskiness. In conjunction with the asset's stable cash flow provision, it works as a moderating factor for the investor's appetite for risk.

Altogether, it can be summarized that the infrastructure asset in this setting comprises three dominant properties. First, it works as a hindering factor for the aim of maximizing the insurance company's net shareholder value due to its illiquidity. Second, its construction period exposes the insurance company to high risks, leading to an incentive for choosing a higher exposure to the risky asset in order to get compensated for the construction costs. Third, after its construction period, it works as a good risk mitigating factor for limiting the portfolio's total risk, because due to its illiquidity, it binds parts of the allocatable capital and hence impedes further investments in the risky asset.

Table 13: Overview of the observed effects on the insurance company's portfolio

Measure \ Variable	mean NSHV	mean default probability	mean solvency ratio	mean SCR fraction	mean risk-free asset's weight	mean risky asset's weight
C-mult.	– –	–	– –	+	-	+
μ_C	–	~	–	+	–	~
σ_C	–	~	–	+	~	~
μ_{OP}	+ +	~	+	–	+	+
σ_{OP}	+	~	–	+	~	~
$w_{B(0)}$	–	–	+	–	+	-
$w_{I(0)}$	– –	–	+	–	–	–
$w_{L(0)}$	–	+	–	–	+	–
δ	~	~	~	~	~	~
w_B^{min}	–	–	+	–	+	-
r(0)	+ +	– –	+	~	–	+
Θ	+	–	+	–	+	+

Source: Own table. The sign + + stands for a strongly increasing effect, + for a lightly increasing effect, – for a lightly decreasing effect, – – for a strongly decreasing effect and ~ for an ambiguous effect. C-mult. denotes the multiple for the construction costs in relation to the first operating cash flow, NSHV the net shareholder value.

The portfolio's solvency capital requirements based on the VaR approach and the standard formula

Figure 6 displays the time depending evolution of the portfolio's solvency capital requirements either determined by the VaR approach as given by equation (29) or by means of the standard formula by equation (43). Thereby, Market-SCR 1 denotes the portfolio's solvency capital requirement as if the infrastructure asset is treated like a type 2 exposure, Market-SCR 2 stands for the SCR if it is treated as a qualifying SPV and Market-SCR 3 for the SCR if it is treated as a qualifying corporate according to the recent advice made by EIOPA. This division emerges in different shock factors applicable to the equity investment in equation (42) in terms of the infrastructure asset's present value.

Since the treatment of the infrastructure asset as a qualifying SPV investment requires the insurance company to apply the lowest shock factor (30 %), it also leads to the lowest solvency capital requirements of all three standard formula approaches over time. Unsurprisingly, the construction period causes relatively high SCRs in the standard formula, because it requires the insurance company to raise its stake in the risky asset in order to get compensated for the losses in equity due to the construction costs. After the construction period, the sharp decline in the risky asset's portfolio weights at periods 4 and 5 (Table 11) causes also a sharp drop in the corresponding capital requirements. These finally begin to raise again as the insurance company continuously increases its stakes in the risky asset and thus incorporates a higher exposure to the equity risk into its portfolio.

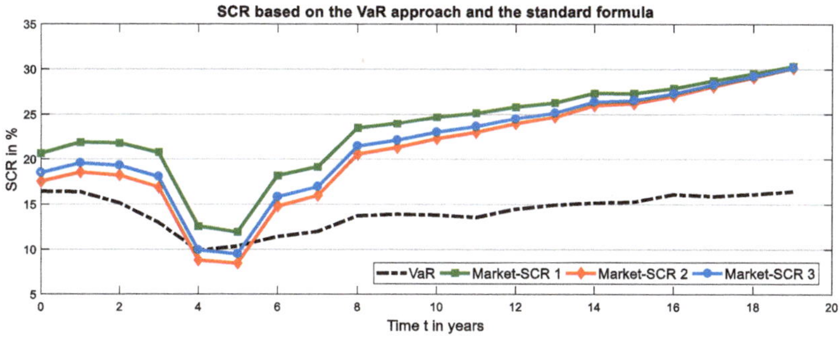

Figure 6: Evolution of the portfolio´s solvency capital requirements (Source: Own figure).

In general, the SCRs determined by the standard formula are consistently overestimated compared to those determined by the VaR approach, except for the periods 4 and 5. Due to the low stakes invested in the risky asset at these periods, the solvency capital requirements need to decline. However, the development of the liabilities, except for the interest rate risk, is not properly addressed and incorporated by the standard formula approach in this setting. The portfolio´s adverse situation of low returns realizable from the risk-free asset due to the low interest rate environment in conjunction with a high riskiness of the risky asset during these periods, while also to be subject to high values of liabilities, is not adequately considered by the amount of the SCR determined by the standard formula.

Although the infrastructure asset´s portfolio weight decreases as its present value continuously shrinks over time (Table 11), the mismatch in the solvency capital requirements between both approaches still increases. This leads to the conclusion that the major part of this deviation must be caused by an overestimation of the risk-free and risky asset´s risk in the standard formula. However, since the sensitivity analysis highlights the infrastructure asset´s general risk reducing behavior, an overestimation of its solvency capital requirements in the standard formula seems to contribute to this overall deviation as well.

As chapters 4.1.2 and 4.3.2 point out, the valuation of the infrastructure asset based on a DCF approach is clearly exposed to the interest rate risk. A comparison between the solvency capital requirements for the infrastructure asset according to its treatment in the equity risk sub-module and in the interest rate risk module shows, however, that the asset´s treatment in the equity risk module leads to consistently higher capital requirements. The differences in the solvency capital requirements between both modules are on average in a range between 36 % and 71 % depending on the asset´s treatment as type 2, qualifying SPV or qualifying corporate. From a risk-oriented perspective, the higher capital requirements for infrastructure assets as treated in the equity risk module like currently implemented under Solvency II are advantageous, since an overestimation of risks leads to a higher safety level of the insurance company. From the perspective of an investor willing to finance infrastructure assets, higher capital requirements than actually necessary work as an additional capital burden and make the investment less valuable. Therefore, it is essential to further scientifically investigate which characteristic of an infrastructure investment, either its exposure to the interest rate risk or to the equity risk, is predominant in order to treat this kind of asset properly from a regulatory and risk-oriented perspective.

4.4 Optimal capital charge for the infrastructure´s sub-module in the equity risk´s module

As the analysis in chapter 4.3.3 points out, there is a distinct difference between the solvency capital requirements for the market risk determined by the VaR approach and by the standard formula. This is not surprising since the standard formula usually tends to overestimate risks due to its design for general applicability among the insurance industry. But in order to narrow this capital gap, and thereby to diminish a potential discrimination of infrastructure assets in terms of their risk contribution to a portfolio, a new risk charge for infrastructure assets is determined in the following section.

4.4.1 Model framework

The proper calibration of the risk charge for infrastructure assets is still in question, as explained in chapter 3.2. However, the adequate risk charge needs to technically ensure that the solvency capital requirement regarding the infrastructure risk meets the 99.5 % percentile of the asset´s loss distribution over one year. This means that the required capital amount needs to cover the potential losses in equity resulting from adverse scenarios in the asset´s market values in 99.5 % of cases over a one-year horizon. According to the general VaR approach provided by equation (44), the solvency capital requirement at time t for the infrastructure asset needs to cover the potential losses in equity resulting from changes in the market values of all assets and liabilities that are exposed to the infrastructure risk.

$$SCR(t)_{infra}^{VaR} := \underset{x}{\operatorname{argmin}} \{P\{A(t)-L(t)-\exp(-r(t,1))\cdot[A(t+1)-L(t+1)]>x\}\leq 1-\alpha\} \quad (44)$$

where: $SCR(t)_{infra}^{VaR}$ denotes the solvency capital requirement at time t based on the VaR approach for the infrastructure asset, P the probability function, A(t) the value of the infrastructure asset at time t, L(t) the value of the liabilities at time t, r(t,1) the one-year risk-free rate at time t as given by the CIR-model and α stands for the confidence interval (99.5 %). The expression within the probability function can be defined as the loss variable.

In order to achieve a representative result and to be independent from the exact composition of the insurance company´s balance sheet, the approach frequently used in literature is applied. If it is assumed that the discounted value of the liabilities at time t+1 equals exactly the value of the liabilities at time t, it results in a cancelation of L(t) and L(t+1) in equation (44).[170] Thus, only the one-year loss in the infrastructure asset´s market value represented by its present value is equivalent to a loss in the equity capital and hence provides the regulatory capital requirement which can be determined by equations (45) and (46).

[170] Cancellation of liabilities in the VaR formula: $-L(t)+\exp(-r(t,1))\cdot L(t+1)=-L(t)+L(t)=0$.

$$SCR(t)_{infra}^{VaR} := \underset{x}{\operatorname{argmin}} \{P\{A(t)\text{-}\exp(\text{-}r(t,1))\cdot A(t+1) > x\} \leq 1\text{-}\alpha\} \quad (45)$$

with

$$SCR(t)_{infra}^{VaR} := \underset{x}{\operatorname{argmin}} \{P\{PV(t)\text{-}\exp(\text{-}r(t,1))\cdot PV(t+1) > x\} \leq 1\text{-}\alpha\} \quad (46)$$

where: $SCR(t)_{infra}^{VaR}$ denotes the solvency capital requirement at time t based on the VaR approach for the infrastructure asset, P the probability function, A(t) the value of the infrastructure asset at time t, L(t) the value of the liabilities at time t, r(t,1) the one-year risk-free rate at time t as given by the CIR-model and α stands for the confidence interval (99.5 %), PV(t) the present value of the infrastructure asset's future and remaining cash flows at time t. The expression within the probability function can be defined as the loss variable.

The determination of the final capital charge for the decline in the market value of the infrastructure asset can be expressed by equation (47). It is assumed to be equivalent to the expected value over the period t = 0 until t = 19 of the 99.5-percentiles of the ratio between the loss in the asset's present value from time t to time t+1 in relation to its present value at time t.

$$s_{infra}^{hyp} = E_{t\epsilon[0;19]}^{P}\left[Q_{99.5}\left(\frac{PV(t)\text{-}\exp(\text{-}r(t,1))\cdot PV(t+1)}{PV(t)}\right)\right] \quad (47)$$

where: s_{infra}^{hyp} stands for hypothetically new risk charge for the infrastructure asset under the standard formula and $Q_{99.5}$ denotes the 99.5-percentile of the infrastructure asset's loss in the market value.

4.4.2 Analysis and findings

Based on this setting, the new capital charge for the infrastructure asset is 15.12 % and hence clearly below the current charges applicable under Solvency II (Table 6). However, this capital charge is in line with EIOPA's statement that empirical data suggest a charge below 20 % for infrastructure assets.[171] Figure 7 shows the evolution of the market solvency capital requirements under application of the new risk charge (Market-SCR new) as well as the former charges for the portfolio's base case scenario. Especially during the early periods, when the infrastructure asset's weight is relatively high, the new risk charge is able to narrow the gap between the SCR determined based on the VaR approach and that determined by means of the standard formula. With respect to the sharp drop in the risky asset's weights at periods 4 and 5, the standard formula's underestimation gains in magnitude, which could lead to a potential danger for the solvency situation of the insurance company. Because this is mainly due to the inappropriate treatment of the liabilities within the standard formula approach underlying this setting, it is likely that the real scope of this deviation will be lower in practice.

However, as the insurance company's investment horizon expires, the infrastructure asset's portfolio weight continuously shrinks and the risky asset's exposure raises. This in turn leads to a further retention of the general mismatch of the solvency capital requirements between both

[171] See EIOPA (2015a), p 14.

approaches, but at least at a slightly lower range, resulting from a more adequate calibration of the infrastructure asset's risk.

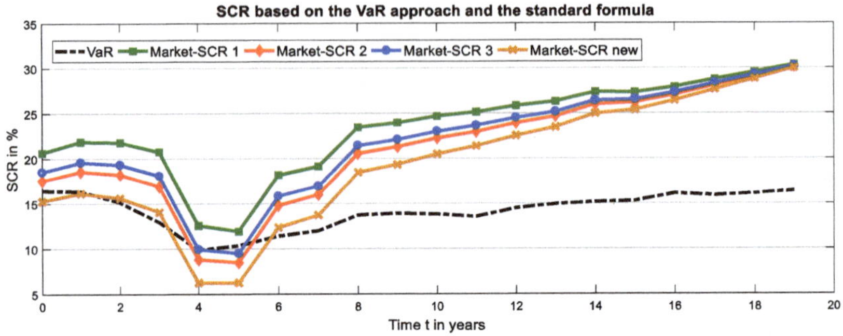

Figure 7: The portfolio's SCR under a new risk charge for the infrastructure asset (Source: Own figure).

5 Discussion of the results

With respect to the results derived from the infrastructure asset´s model and the setting of the insurance company´s portfolio, there are several issues with a general impact on the quality of the inferred insights. The following discussion, however, only comprises the most important aspects.

At first, the composition and the design of the assets and liabilities needs to be improved with the aim of illustrating a more representative balance sheet of an insurance company. Especially the liability side, which is in reality extremely complex, needs to be designed in a more detailed manner for simulation purposes in order to reflect its influence on the company´s solvency situation more adequately. Thereby, the exact dynamics of the interdependency between an infrastructure asset as a long-term investment and the liabilities as usually long-term obligations, are still unclear and of particular importance, especially in the context of narrowing the duration gap. Considering the risk mitigating behavior of the infrastructure asset in this setting, its positive influence on the portfolio´s solvency situation needs to be assessed against the background of liabilities with a changing long-term exposure.

Regarding the infrastructure asset´s valuation model, the main troubling issue is the prevailing lack of sufficient market data for a proper calibration of the model´s parameters. Although the market for direct infrastructure assets is still emerging and not standardized yet (chapter 2), there is already a growing interest of institutional investors like the insurance or banking industry in investing in that asset class, leading to a growing number of investment deals. Therefore, the potential of generating market data is already existent, but any access to that data for research purposes is currently limited. Both, the private as well as public side, do not provide data in a sufficient manner which leads to the current problem of circularity. As long as there is no sufficient data for the purpose of research, the risk-return profiles of infrastructure asset´s cannot be adequately scientifically assessed, which impedes its proper regulatory treatment that in turn bears the risk of making the entire asset class unattractive for institutional investors. Hence, it avoids the further emergence of the infrastructure market and the potential for generating the urgently needed market data. However, better and more realistic calibrations of the infrastructure assets´ valuation models help to identify the assets´ true impact on the performance and solvency situation of an insurance company´s portfolio and hence provide the foundation to justify an adequate regulatory capital charge (chapter 4.4.2).

Besides the difficulty of the model´s right calibration, its general break down into three individual cash flow streams seems to deliver economically sound results. However, it could be interesting to introduce a salvage value at the end of the decommissioning phase instead of the implemented assumption of the asset´s complete worthlessness. Due to the longer impact of the asset´s illiquidity constraint, it is likely that the insurance company extends the increase in the risky asset´s stake over a longer period, while holding the risk-free asset´s weight at its minimum bound. This in turn leads to significantly different outcomes for the portfolio´s performance, its solvency situation and the resulting capital requirements, since larger amounts of the allocatable funds are bound by the infrastructure asset. This setting would emphasize the ambiguous role of the asset´s illiquidity constraint as on the one hand, performance reducing, but on the other hand, as risk mitigating.

In a following step, the illiquidity constraint should be relaxed, for instance, by allowing the insurance company to sell and buy stakes of the infrastructure asset within a certain range. This could be realized in practice when considering the infrastructure asset in this setting as a portfolio consisting of strongly positive correlated individual infrastructure assets. This seems to be helpful in order to disentangle and to distinguish between the exact impact of the asset's stable cash flow provision and its illiquidity constraint on the portfolio's overall performance and solvency situation.

Finally, the current treatment of infrastructure assets under the standard formula of Solvency II leads to several unclear issues. Due to the immaturity of the Delegated Regulation (EU) 2016/467 and the resulting introduction of several qualifying criteria for infrastructure investments in the equity risk module (chapter 3.2), it is currently not possible to assess the practicability of these criteria. Since there are many complaints from the insurance industry with respect to the criteria's scope, it could be the case that these requirements impose an inappropriate safety condition in addition to the solvency capital requirement. Thus, their appropriateness need to be investigated from an investor's perspective in order to justify their existence. Furthermore, the calibration of the regulatory capital charge and the approach used by EIOPA to derive it, are still questionable and need to incorporate the general influence of market movements due to differences in the assets' valuation approaches by means of quoted market prices and appraisal-based techniques (chapters 2.2 and 3.2). In addition, the result of the capital charge derived in chapter 4.2 further underpins the need for a review.

Although the underlying setting shows that the treatment of the infrastructure asset within the equity risk module is adequate from a risk-oriented perspective (chapter 4.3.3), it is still not clear to which extent the asset's exposure to the interest rate risk, especially in conjunction with a DCF approach for the asset's valuation, can be justified in practice (chapters 2.2 and 3.2). However, in order to provide more evidence, sufficient market data need to be gathered in future.

6 Conclusion

The market for infrastructure investments can still be seen as immature and non-standardized, mainly resulting from the high degree of heterogeneity of the infrastructure asset class. However, the analysis of the market potential points out a large investment gap as well as four major trends that are likely to further raise the global need for infrastructure investments and emphasize the market´s general capability of providing promising investment opportunities for institutional investors in future.

The past performance of direct infrastructure assets underpin their ability to provide stable and long-term cash flows, relatively high and stable returns, high diversification benefits as well as low systematic risk levels of the underlying infrastructure business models and only modest marginal default rates. But with regard to their potential risk sources, the analysis points out a time-variant occurrence of specific risk types according to the four usual apparent lifecycle phases, leading to severe differences in the risk exposures for investors. However, due to the heterogeneity of the entire sub asset-class, the insights about the risk-return profiles differ significantly for each infrastructure asset and cannot be generalized.

Considering the regulatory treatment of direct infrastructure investments under Solvency II, there has been recent changes through the introduction of the Delegated Regulation (EU) 2016/467 that implemented a tailored asset class for qualifying equity infrastructure investments under the standard formula. Thereby, it is currently possible for insurance companies to treat their direct infrastructure assets within the equity risk module as either type 2 exposures (49 % capital charge) or in case of a compliance with several qualifying criteria, as qualifying project investments (30 % capital charge). In June 2016, EIOPA published an additional advice of introducing a further asset class for a tailored treatment of investments in qualifying infrastructure corporates. However, the practicability of the qualifying criteria and the adequateness of the current capital charges as well as of the correlation coefficients remain open.

The developed infrastructure model for determining the current market value of an infrastructure asset in this setting delivers sound economic results. It takes the three most important lifecycle phases into account and is consistent with the J-curve effect of the cumulative cash flows typically apparent for infrastructure assets. Furthermore, it highlights the magnitude of the risk stemming from the construction phase that is able to not only jeopardize the asset´s individual performance, but also to exert a strong influence on the performance and safety level of an underlying institutional portfolio.

Thereby, the insurance company in this setting aims to maximize its net shareholder value over a time horizon of 20 years and under consideration of a solvency, a weight and an illiquidity constraint imposed by the infrastructure asset. The results highlight a trade-off situation between the aim to maximize the net shareholder value and to lower the insurance company´s overall risk. Furthermore, especially the construction phase provides an incentive for the insurance company to increase its stake in the risky asset in order to get compensated for the loss in equity caused by the high level of construction costs.

From the perspective of the portfolio´s solvency capital requirements determined by the VaR approach and by means of the standard formula under Solvency II, a comparison of both requirements depicts a general overestimation of the standard formula. The construction phase, in particular, is in both approaches a main driver for the portfolio´s overall risk level during the early periods of the investment horizon and deteriorates its solvency situation clearly. A comparison of the solvency capital requirements for the infrastructure asset under the treatment of both, the standard formula´s equity risk`s and interest rate risk`s sub-modules, results in higher capital requirements for the equity risk exposure.

Finally, the determination of an own capital charge for the infrastructure asset underlying this setting leads to a new capital charge of 15.1 %, which is consistent with the upper bound stated by EIOPA. However, the application of this capital charge is not able to close completely the gap between the solvency capital requirements determined by the VaR approach and the standard formula, but it narrows it. Thus, this lower capital charge argues in favor of a further lowering of the regulatory capital charge for direct infrastructure assets.

In summary, considering an insurance company as a risk-averse investor, the infrastructure asset in this setting can be recommended for an investment purpose, because it improves the insurance company´s entire solvency situation by lowering its default probability and increasing its solvency ratio, which is regarded as worthwhile aim. Under consideration of the literature´s empirical results about direct infrastructure assets, this assessment gains in further relevance. But besides the general soundness of the outcomes and rationales identified by this setting, it is worth noting that the lack of market data regarding infrastructure assets imposes a strong limitation on the generalization of the findings. Therefore, it is absolutely necessary to generate a higher amount of data in future in order to raise the quality of these first insights about the performance of direct infrastructure assets within an insurance company´s portfolio.

List of References

Albrecht, P. / Maurer, R. (2008): "Investment- und Risikomanagement", Third edition, Schäffer-Poeschel Verlag, Stuttgart.

Ammar, S. B. / Eling, M. (2015): "Common risk factors of infrastructure investments", Energy Economics, 49, May 2015, pp. 257-273.

AMP Capital (2014): "Infrastructure Investment: Combining Listed With Unlisted", Industry report, AMP Capital, Sydney.

AustralianSuper (2013): "Fact Sheet: Comparing listed and unlisted assets", Industry Report, AustralianSuper, Melbourne.

Bahceci, S. / Weisdorf, M. (2014): "The Investment Characteristics of OECD Infrastructure: A Cash-Flow Analysis", Rotman International Journal of Pension Management, 7 (1), pp. 32-39.

Bauer, D. / Reuss, A. / Singer, D. (2012): "On the Calculation of the Solvency Capital Requirement Based on Nested Simulations", ASTIN Bulletin, 42 (2), pp. 453-499.

Berdin, E. / Sottocornola, M. (2015): "Insurance Activities and Systemic Risk", Working paper, ICIR Working Paper Series, 15 (19), pp. 1-54.

Berger, A. N. / Cummins, D. J. / Weiss, M. A. (1997): "The Coexistence of Multiple Distribution Systems for Financial Services: The Case of Property-Liability Insurance", The Journal of Business, 70 (4), pp. 515-546.

Bing, L. / Akintoye, A. / Edwards, P.J. / Hardcastle, C. (2005): "The allocation of risk in PPP/PFI construction projects in the UK", International Journal of Project Management, 23 (1), pp. 25-35.

Bird, R. / Liem, H. / Thorp, S. (2014): "Infrastructure: Real Assets and Real Returns", European Financial Management, 20 (4), pp. 802-824.

Bitsch, F. (2012): "Cash Flow Stability Versus Transparency: What do Investors Value about Listed Infrastructure Funds?", in: Choi, J. J. / Sami, H. (Ed.), "Transparency and Governance in a Global World", International Finance Review, Volume 13, pp. 199-229.

Bitsch, F. / Buchner, A. / Kaserer, C. (2010): "Risk, return and cash flow characteristics of infrastructure fund investments", EIB papers, 15 (1), pp. 106-136.

Björk, T. (2009): "Arbitrage Theory in Continuous Time", Third edition, Oxford University Press, Oxford.

Blanc-Brude, F. (2013): "Towards Efficient Benchmarks for Infrastructure Equity Investments", Working paper, EDHEC-Risk Institute Publication, Paris.

Brigo, D. / Dalessandro, A. / Neugebauer, M. / Triki, F. (2009): "A stochastic process toolkit for risk management: Geometric brownian motion, jumps, garch and variance gamma models", Journal of Risk Management in Financial Institutions, 2 (4), pp. 365-393.

Brigo, D. / Mercurio, F. (2006): "Interest rate models-theory and practice: with sile, inflation and credit", Second edition, Springer, Berlin.

Bundesanstalt für Finanzdienstleistungsaufsicht (BaFin) (2015): "Vorbereitung auf Solvency II: Berechnung der Solvabilitätskapitalanforderung (SCR)", Guideline document, BaFin, Bonn.

Börger, M. (2010): "Deterministic shock vs. stochastic value-at-risk - an analysis of the Solvency II standard model approach to longevity risk", Blätter der DGVFM, 31 (2), pp. 225-259.

Canning, D. / Pedroni, P. (2008): "Infrastructure, Long-Run Economic Growth And Causality Tests For Cointegrated Panels", The Manchester School, 76 (5), pp. 504-527.

Checherita-Westphal, C. / Rother, P. (2012): "The impact of high government debt on economic growth and its channels: An empirical investigation for the euro area", European Economic Review, 56 (7), pp. 1392-1405.

Christiansen, M. C. / Niemeyer, A. (2012): "The fundamental definition of the Solvency Capital Requirement in Solvency II", Working paper, University Ulm, pp. 1-26.

Cox, J. C. / Ingersoll, J. E. J. / Ross, S. A. (1985): "A theory of the term structure of interest rates", Econometrica, 53 (2), pp. 385-407.

Deutsche Bundesbank (2014): "Financial Stability Review 2014", Industry report, Deutsche Bundes-bank, Frankfurt/Main.

Ehlers, T. (2014): "Understanding the challenges for infrastructure finance", BIS working papers, No 454, Bank for International Settlements, Basel.

Ernst & Young (EY) (2015): "Infrastructure Investments: An attractive to help deliver a prosperous and sustainable economy", Industry report, PricewaterhouseCoopers, London.

Esfahani, H. S. / Ramírez, M. T. (2003): "Institutions, infrastructure, and economic growth", Journal of Development Economics, 70 (2), pp. 443-477.

Espinoza, D. / Morris, J. (2013): "Decoupled NPV: a simple, improved method to value infrastructure investments", Construction Management and Economics, 31 (5), pp. 471-496.

European Commission (2014): "Communication From The Commission To The European Parliament And The Council on Long-Term Financing of the European Economy", Communique, European Commission, Brussels.

European Commission (2015): "Solvency II Overview – Frequently asked questions", Fact sheet, European Commission, Brussels.

European Insurance and Occupational Pensions Authority (EIOPA) (2011): "EIOPA Report on the fifth Quantitative Impact Study (QIS 5) for Solvency II", Study, EIOPA, Frankfurt/Main.

European Insurance and Occupational Pensions Authority (EIOPA) (2014a): "The underlying assumptions in the standard formula for the Solvency Capital Requirement calculation", Guideline document, EIOPA, Frankfurt/Main.

European Insurance and Occupational Pensions Authority (EIOPA) (2014b): "Technical Specification for the Preparatory Phase (Part I)", Guideline document, EIOPA, Frankfurt/Main.

European Insurance and Occupational Pensions Authority (EIOPA) (2015a): "Final Report on Consultation Paper no. 15/004", Report published on 29 September 2015, EIOPA, Frankfurt/Main.

European Insurance and Occupational Pensions Authority (EIOPA) (2015b): "Guidelines on the treatment of market and counterparty risk exposures in the standard formula", Guideline document, EIOPA, Frankfurt/Main.

European Insurance and Occupational Pensions Authority (EIOPA) (2015c): "Guidelines on recognition and valuation of assets and liabilities other than technical provisions", Guideline document, EIOPA, Frankfurt/Main.

European Insurance and Occupational Pensions Authority (EIOPA) (2016a): "Final Report on Consultation Paper no. 16/004", Report published on 30 June 2016, EIOPA, Frankfurt/Main.

European Insurance and Occupational Pensions Authority (EIOPA) (2016b): "Technical Advice on the identification and calibration of infrastructure investments risk categories, i.e. infrastructure corporates", Guideline document, EIOPA, Frankfurt/Main.

European PPP Expertise Center (2016): "Market Update: Review of the European PPP Market in 2015", Industry report, European Investment Bank, Luxembourg.

European Systemic Risk Board (ESRB) (2015): "ESRB report on the regulatory treatment of sovereign exposures", Study, ESRB, Frankfurt/Main.

European Union (2012): Regulation (EU) No 670/2012, European Parliament and the Council, Brussels.

Eurostat (2016a): Statistics about general government gross debt, statistics code: teina225 http://ec.europa.eu/eurostat/tgm/table.do?tab=table&init=1&language=en&pcode=teina225&plugin= (last access: 10 May 2016).

Eurostat (2016b): Statistics about general government gross debt, Indicator: Interest, payable, statistics code: gov_10dd_edpt1, http://appsso.eurostat.ec.europa.eu/nui/submitViewTableAction.do (last ac-cess: 10 May 2016).

Finkenzeller, K. / Dechant, T. / Schäfers, W. (2010): "Infrastructure: A new dimension of real estate? An asset allocation analysis", Journal of Property Investment and Finance, 28 (4), pp. 263-274.

Fischer, K. / Schlütter, S. (2014): "Optimal Investment Strategies for Insurance Companies when Capital Requirements are imposed by a Standard Formula", Working paper, ICIR working paper series, 12 (09), pp. 1-32.

Flyvbjerg, B. / Holm, M. K. / Buhl, S. (2003): "How common and how large are cost overruns in transport infrastructure projects?", Transport Reviews, 23 (1), pp. 71-88.

Gatzert, N. / Kosub, T. (2014): "Insurers′ Investment in Infrastructure: Overview and Treatment under Solvency II", The Geneva Papers, 39 (2), pp. 351-372.

Gatzert, N. / Martin, M. (2012): "Quantifying Credit and Market Risk under Solvency II: Standard Approach versus Internal Model", Working paper, University of Erlangen-Nürnberg, pp. 1-47.

Grimsey, D. / Lewis, M. K. (2002): "Evaluating the risks of public private partnerships for infrastructure projects", International Journal of Project Management, 20 (2), pp. 107-118.

Hartigan, L. R. / Prasad, R. / De Francesco, A. (2011): "Constructing an investment return series for the UK unlisted infrastructure market: estimation and application", Journal of Property Research, 28 (1), pp. 35-58.

Ho, S. P. / Liu, L. Y. (2002): "An option pricing-based model for evaluating the financial viability of privatized infrastructure projects", Construction Management and Economics, 20 (2), pp. 143-156.

Humphreys, T. / Maclean, G. / Rogers, J. (2016): "Equity Infrastructure Valuations: Leads, Lags And Controversies", Industry report, AMP Capital, Sydney.

Inderst, G. (2010): "Infrastructure as an asset class", EIB Papers, 15 (1), pp. 70-104.

Insurance Europe (2015a): "European Insurance – Key Facts: August 2015", Industry report, Insurance Europe, Brussels.

Insurance Europe (2015b): "Response to EIOPA consultation on the identification and calibration of infrastructure corporates", Position Paper, Insurance Europe, Brussels.

Jeong, J. / Ji, C. / Hong, T. / Park, H. S. (2016): "Model for Evaluating the Financial Viability of the BOT Project for Highway Service Areas in South Korea", Journal of Management in Engineering, 32 (2), pp. 1-13.

Jorgenson, D. W. / Vu, K. M. (2013): "The emergence of the new economic order: Growth in the G7 and the G20", Journal of Policy Modeling, 35 (3), pp. 389-399.

Kikeri, S. / Nellis, J. (2004): "An Assessment of Privatization", The World Bank Research Observer, 19 (1), pp. 87-118.

Kleine, J. / Schulz, T. C. / Krautbauer, M. (2012): "Rendite- und Risiko-Profile bei Eigen- und Fremdkapitalinvestitionen in Infrastruktur", Research study, Steinbeis Research Center for Financial Services, Munich.

Kleine, J. / Schulz, T. C. / Krautbauer, M. (2015): "Infrastrukturinvestments – Übersicht über eigen- und fremdkapitalbasierte Anlagemöglichkeiten", in: Kleine, J. / Schulz, T. C. / Krautbauer, M. (Ed.), "Infrastrukturinvestments", Springer Gabler, Wiesbaden, pp. 81-100.

Loosemore, M. (2007): "Risk allocation in the private provision of public infrastructure", International Journal of Project Management, 25 (1), pp. 66-76.

Martin, M. (2013): "Assessing the model risk with respect to the interest rate term structure under Solvency II", The Journal of Risk Finance, 14 (3), pp. 200-233.

McHugh, M. / Schiffel, S. (2014): "Omnibus II agreement on long-term guarantee package and transitional measures", Industry report, Munich Re, Munich.

McKinsey Global Institute (MGI) (2013): "Infrastructure productivity: How to save $1 trillion a year", Industry report, McKinsey & Company, New York.

Moody´s (2013): "Default and Recovery Rates for Project Finance Bank Loans, 1983-2011", Industry report, Moody´s Investors Service, New York.

Newell, G. / Peng, H. W. (2008): "The Role of U.S. Infrastructure in Investment Portfolios", Journal of Real Estate Portfolio Management, 14 (1), pp. 21-33.

Newell, G. / Peng, H. W. / De Francesco, A. (2011): "The performance of unlisted infrastructure in investment portfolios", Journal of Property Research, 28 (1), pp. 59-74.

Niedrig, T. (2015): "Optimal Asset Allocation for Interconnected Life Insurers in the Low Interest Rate Environment under Solvency Regulation", Journal of Insurance Issues, 38 (1), pp. 31-71.

Niedrig, T. / Gründl, H. (2015): "The Effects of Contingent Convertible (CoCo) Bonds on Insurers´ Capital Requirements under Solvency II", Working paper, ICIR working paper series, 14 (18), pp. 1-35.

Nieuwerburgh, S. V. / Stanton, R. / Bever, L. d. (2015): "A review of real estate and infrastructure investments by the Norwegian Government Pension Fund Global (GPFG)", Study, GPFG, Oslo.

Organisation for Economic Co-operation and Development (OECD) (2007): "Infrastructure to 2030: Mapping Policy for Electricity, Water and Transport", Volume 2, OECD Publications, Paris.

Organisation for Economic Co-operation and Development (OECD) (2015): "Annual Survey of Large Pension Funds and Public Pension Reserve Funds", OECD, Paris.

Organisation for Economic Co-operation and Development (OECD) (2016a), Statistics about social expenditure, https://stats.oecd.org/Index.aspx?DataSetCode=SOCX_AGG (last access: 20 May 2016).

Organisation for Economic Co-operation and Development (OECD) (2016b), Statistics about the inflation rate (CPI): https://data.oecd.org/price/inflation-cpi.htm#indicator-chart, the inflation rate forecast: https://data.oecd.org/price/inflation-forecast.htm, and the unit labor costs: https://data.oecd.org/lprdty/unit-labour-costs.htm (last access: 20 May 2016).

Organisation for Economic Co-operation and Development (OECD) (2016c), Statistics about the GDP growth rate, https://data.oecd.org/gdp/real-gdp-forecast.htm (last access: 20 May 2016).

Oyedele, J. B. / Adair, A. / McGreal, S. (2014): "Performance of global listed infrastructure investment in a mixed asset portfolio", Journal of Property Research, 31 (1), pp. 1-25.

Peng, H. W. / Newell, G. (2007): "The Significance Of Infrastructure In Australian Investment Portfolios", Pacific Rim Property Research Journal, 13 (4), pp. 423-450.

Preqin (2016a): "Q1 2016 Infrastructure Deals", Data fact sheet, Preqin, London.

Preqin (2016b): "Preqin Investor Outlook: Alternative Assets H1 2016", Industry report, Preqin, London.

PricewaterhouseCoopers (PwC) (2013): "Capital project and infrastructure spending: Outlook to 2025", Industry report, PricewaterhouseCoopers, London.

PricewaterhouseCoopers (PwC) (2015): "The world in 2050: Will the shift in global economic power continue?", Industry report, PricewaterhouseCoopers, London.

Rojas, A. / Tubio, B. (2015): "Spain′s renewable energy regime: Challenges and uncertainties", SEFO – Spanish Economic and Financial Outlook, 4 (2), pp. 57-66.

Rothballer, C. / Kaserer, C. (2012): "The Risk Profile of Infrastructure Investments: challenging Con-ventional Wisdom", The Journal of Structured Finance, 18 (2), pp. 95-109.

Sanchez-Robles, B. (1998): "Infrastructure Investment and Growth: Some Empirical Evidence", Contemporary Economic Policy, 16 (1), pp. 98-108.

Schaufelberger, J. E. / Wipadapisut, I. (2003): "Alternate Financing Strategies for Build-Operate-Transfer Projects", Journal of Construction Engineering and Management, 129 (2), pp. 205-213.

The Guardian (2016): "Norway′s oil-based wealth fund sells out of more fossil fuel companies", https://www.theguardian.com/environment/2016/feb/05/norways-wealth-fund-sells-out-of-73-companies-as-fossil-fears-grow (last access: 25 May 2016).

United Nations (UN) (2015): "World Population Ageing", Economic and social affairs report, United Nations, New York.

van Hulle, K. (2011): "Solvency II: state of play and perspectives", Zeitschrift für die gesamte Versicherungswissenschaft, 100 (2), pp. 177-192.

Wibowo, A. / Alfen, H. W. (2013): "Fine-tuning the value and cost of capital of risky PPP infrastructure projects", Engineering, Construction and Architectural Management, 20 (4), pp. 406-419.

World Economic Forum (WEF) (2012): "Strategic Infrastructure", Industry report, World Economic Forum publication, Geneva.

Zhang, X. (2005): "Financial Viability Analysis and Capital Structure Optimization in Privatized Public Infrastructure Projects", Journal of Construction Engineering and Management, 131 (6), pp. 656-668.

Appendix

A.1 Cholesky decomposition technique[172]

For the variance-covariance matrix A, it holds:

$$\rho_{A,B} = \frac{cov(r_A, r_B)}{\sigma_A \cdot \sigma_B} \xrightarrow{yields} cov(r_A, r_B) = \rho_{A,B} \cdot \sigma_A \cdot \sigma_B$$

Modeling correlated asset returns is mainly based on the simulation of correlated normally distributed random variables. The approach mostly used is the Cholesky decomposition of the asset´s variance-covariance matrix. Thereby, the variance-covariance matrix is decomposed into a lower and upper triangular matrix. The product of the lower triangular matrix with a vector of i.i.d. standard normally distributed variables provides a vector of correlated variables satisfying the former covariance matrix. Denoting H the lower triangular matrix of A (the variance-covariance matrix of the assets) and Z the vector of i.i.d. standard normal variables, then the vector C represents correlated random variables.

$$H \cdot \vec{Z} = \vec{C}$$

Therefore, for correlating the Brownian motions underlying the assets, the liabilities and the short rate in this setting, it holds for the correlated GBM´s

$$dS_i(t) = m_i S(t) dt + S_i(t) H dW_i(t)$$

with

$$m_i = \mu_i - \frac{\sigma_i^2}{2}$$

and for the CIR process:

$$dr(t) = [k\theta - (k + \lambda\sigma_r) r(t)] dt + \sqrt{r(t)} H dW_r(t)$$

And discretized:

$$S_i(t) = S_i(t-1) \cdot \exp((\mu_i - \frac{\sigma_i^2}{2}) \Delta t + C_i \sqrt{\Delta t})$$

$$r(t) = r(t-1) + k(\theta - r(t-1)) \Delta t + C_r \sqrt{\Delta t \cdot r(t-1)}$$

172 In accordance with Albrecht/Maurer (2008), pp. 196-200.

A.2 Calibration of the risky asset with respect to the DAX

Parameter	Value	Calculus
Average monthly log return μ_m	0.006767652	ln[S(t)/S(t-1)]
Annualized monthly log return $\mu_{p.a.}$	0.081211827	$\mu_{p.a.}=\mu_m \cdot 12$
Monthly standard deviation σ_m	0.061051236	Standard deviation of monthly log-returns
Annualized standard deviation $\sigma_{p.a.}$	0.211487685	$\sigma_{p.a.}=\sigma_m \cdot \sqrt{12}$
Time period	01/1991 - 12/2015	end of month data

Source: Own Table. Data derived from Yahoo! Finance.

A.3 Overview of the parameters and their calibration used in the simulation (Part I)

Parameter	Calibration	Comment
Construction phase´s time period t	$t \in [1,3]$	-
Operating phase´s time period t	$t \in [4,15]$	-
Decommissioning phase time period t	$t \in [16,20]$	-
Number of simulation paths	10 000	-
Construction cost-multiple	2.0	Multiple of the starting value for the first construction costs C(0) in relation to the first operating cash flow $CF^{OP}(0)$.
μ_C	4% p.a.	Drift coefficient of the construction costs. Explained in section 4.1.
σ_C	10 % p.a.	Volatility coefficient of the construction costs. Explained in section 4.1.
$CF^{OP}(0)$	25 units	Assumption.
μ_{OP}	6 % p.a.	Drift coefficient of the operating cash flows. Explained in section 4.1.
σ_{OP}	7 % p.a.	Volatility coefficient of the operating cash flows. Explained in section 4.1.
μ_D	2 % p.a.	Drift coefficient of the decommissioning cash flows. Explained in section 4.1.
σ_D	7 % p.a.	Volatility coefficient of the decommissioning cash flows. Explained in section 4.1.

Overview of the parameters and their calibration used in the simulation (Part II)

Parameter	Calibration	Comment
$CF^{D}(0) = CF^{D}(16)$	$CF^{OP}(15)$	Starting value for the process of the decommissioning cash flows is the last incoming cash flow from the operating phase, $CF^{OP}(15)$.
k	10.36 % p.a.	Speed of the process´ reversion to the long-term value.
Θ	5 % p.a.	Long-term value of the short rate. Explained in section 4.2.
σ_r	3.9 % p.a.	Volatility of the short rate. Explained in section 4.2.
r(0)	1% p.a.	Starting value for the short rate´s process. Explained in section 4.2.
λ	0	Factor for the market risk. Assumed to be zero. Explained in section 4.2.
μ_S	8 % p.a.	Drift coefficient of the risky asset, representing the DAX. Explained in section 4.2.
σ_S	21 % p.a.	Volatility coefficient of the risky asset, representing the DAX. Explained in section 4.2.
μ_L	1 % p.a.	Drift coefficient of the liabilities. Explained in section 4.2.
σ_L	5 % p.a.	Volatility coefficient of the liabilities. Explained in section 4.2.
$w_{B(0)}$	72 %	Initial portfolio weight for the risk-free asset.
$w_{S(0)}$	18 %	Initial portfolio weight for the risky asset.
$w_{I(0)}$	10 %	Initial portfolio weight for the infrastructure asset according to suggestions from the literature. Explained in section 4.3.
$w_{L(0)}$	80 %	Initial portfolio weight for the liabilities.
δ	20 %	Maximum change of portfolio weights per period for risky and safe asset.
w_B^{min}	70 %	Minimum portfolio weight for the risk-free asset at every period t.
w_S^{max}	30 %	Maximum portfolio weight for the risky asset at every period t.
$s_{infra,j}$	49 % / 30 % / 36 %	Shock factors under the standard formula of Solvency II regarding the infrastructure asset´s treatment as either a type 2 exposure / SPV / corporate.

Source: Own Table.

A.4 Overview of the correlation coefficients of the market risk´s module under the standard formula of Solvency II

	Interest rate	Equity	Property	Spread	Concentration	Currency
Interest rate	1	A	A	A	0	0.25
Equity	A	1	0.75	0.75	0	0.25
Property	A	0.75	1	0.5	0	0.25
Spread	A	0.75	0.5	1	0	0.25
Concentration	0	0	0	0	1	0
Currency	0.25	0.25	0.25	0.25	0	1

Source: Own Table, based on: Delegated Regulation (EU) 2015/35, section 5, subsection 1 (164).

A is equal to 0 (0.5) if the capital requirement for the interest rate risk is based on an upward (downward) shock scenario for the term structure of interest rates.

Kolibri 360 GmbH
Ferdinand-Jühlke-Straße 7
99095 Erfurt, Deutschland
produktsicherheit@kolibri360.de